PRAISE FOR PEGGY F
THE LONG PROGRAM

"A feel-good memoir . . . As Fleming tells about making the transition from champion skater to television star to ABC commentator, she displays the same effortless grace off and on the ice."

—*Chicago Sun-Times*

"What makes Fleming's autobiography appealing is her confidence and philosophy toward sports and life. . . . She is adept at delicately broaching awkward, sad, and uncomfortable subjects that would make most people wince."

—*Los Angeles Times*

"This is both an autobiography and a life plan for young women as they segue from youth to maturity. . . . Offers large dollops of common sense, inspiration, and perspiration. There aren't any better role models for women than Fleming."

—*Booklist*

"Readers will learn about Fleming personally. . . . She's quite honest, even when discussing painful subjects."

—*Publishers Weekly*

"A fascinating and intimate memoir."

—*Abilene Reporter-News* (TX)

"A fun trip down memory lane."

—*Grand Rapids Press* (MI)

PEGGY FLEMING

with Peter Kaminsky

THE LONG PROGRAM

Skating Toward Life's Victories

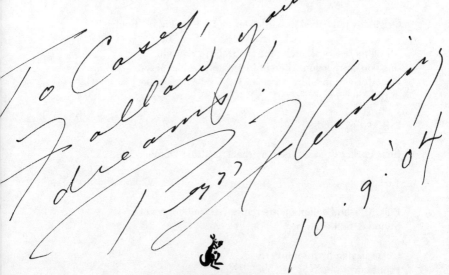

To Casey,
Fallow your
dreams!
Peggy Fleming
10.9.'04

POCKET BOOKS

New York   London   Toronto   Sydney   Singapore

POCKET BOOKS, a division of Simon & Schuster, Inc.
1230 Avenue of the Americas, New York, NY 10020

Copyright © 1999 by Peggy Fleming, Inc.

Originally published in hardcover in 1999 by Pocket Books

All rights reserved, including the right to reproduce
this book or portions thereof in any form whatsoever.
For information address Pocket Books, 1230 Avenue
of the Americas, New York, NY 10020

ISBN: 0-671-03887-7

First Pocket Books trade paperback printing October 2000

10   9   8   7   6   5   4   3   2   1

POCKET and colophon are registered trademarks of
Simon & Schuster, Inc.

Cover design by Joseph Perez
Front cover photo by Michael O'Neill

Printed in the U.S.A.

For my mom, whose strength, determination, and love carried me to a gold medal. I miss you and love you.

And for Greg, my greatest friend, greatest love, and greatest support. Your steady hand held mine through every step of this journey. Thank you for finding me and making me complete.

Free Skating Program
1968 Olympic Winter Games, Grenoble, France
Choreography by Bob Paul
Drawn by Peggy Fleming

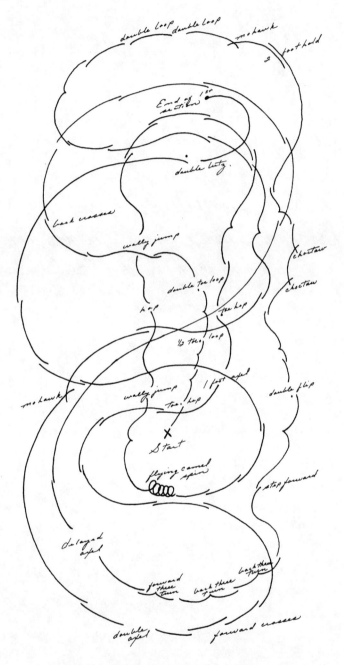

double loop   double loop   mohawk
2 foot hold
End of 1st section
double lutz
back crosses
wally jump
choctaw
choctaw
double toe loop
toe hop
toe hop
½ toe loop
mohawk   wally jump   1 foot axel   double flip
toe hop
X
Start
flying camel spin
step forward
delayed axel
forward three turn   back three turn   back three turn
double axel   forward crosses

Symphony No.6 "Pathétique"—Tchaikovsky

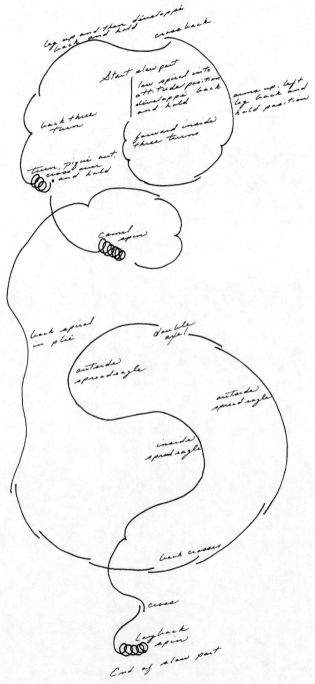

Samson and Delilah—Saint-Saëns

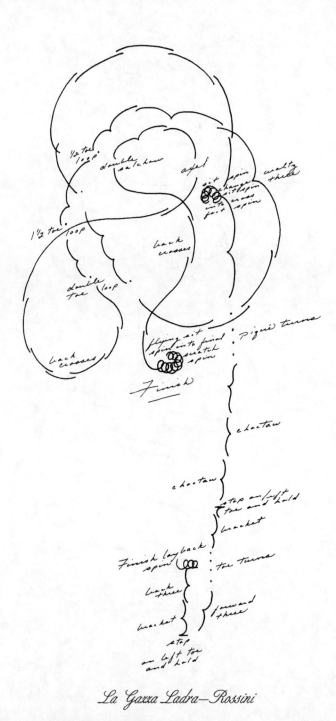

½ toe loop

double salchow

axel

sit spin change to sit flip spin into arms foot spin

waltz three

1½ toe loop

back crosses

double toe loop

back crosses

flying sit spin into final scratch spin

Pigeon turns

Finish

chactaw

chactaw

step on left toe and hold

bracket

Finish layback spin

toe turns

back three

forward three

bracket

step on left toe and hold

La Gazza Ladra—Rossini

CONTENTS

The Long Program

Life, Art, Sports, and Me

*L*ast year I turned fifty, became a grand-mother, fought breast cancer, and remodeled my kitchen. I've been busy.

The events of the past twelve months quite naturally led me to take a long look at my life: There's nothing like a wake-up call to your mortality to help you take the measure of where you've been and where you want to end up.

In skating, the thing that wins you a medal is your Long Program. It's a carefully crafted series of jumps, spins, and moves that you plan out to show off your best qualities. You practice it until it is all you think of throughout the day and then you dream of it all night. You practice until everything comes together as naturally as breathing, and you hope you get it right when it counts. But until you hit the ice, until you feel if it is rough or smooth, fast or slow; until you see the looks in the judges' eyes; until you feel the energy of the crowd wash over you, it's fair to say you don't have a clue how it's all going to turn out. You just have to do it and see where your Long Program takes you.

Whether it's those few minutes on the ice, or life in general, I believe we all have a Long Program: those precious years that take little girls and make them into wives, mothers, grandmas, and survivors. We all have goals, and we all take different steps to get us there, but whether life's ice is chewed up or like glass, whether the crowd is kind or hostile, whether you feel sick or fit, it is only by living each moment that we learn how things will turn out. You can be sure of only one thing—there will be surprises. Making a plan and then reacting to the twists and turns of reality is what skating is all about and what life is all about.

Having been a serious skater for most of my childhood and an athlete of sorts almost from the day I could walk, you would think that I knew exactly where my own Long Program was taking me, but that wasn't—and probably still isn't—the case. There have always been surprises on the ice and off. The four minutes that won me a gold medal in Grenoble in 1968 at the Olympic Winter Games were that kind of surprise. On the one hand they were just another competition, in many ways no different from the dozens of competitions I had skated and, for the most part, won for nearly ten years. On the other hand in 1968, in the midst of the tumultuous 1960s, the Olympics were much more than just another event. It was a time of rebellion, questioning of values, drugs, and protest, and there was something reassuring and attractive about a global gathering of youth, all with a direction and purpose, all young and beautiful, clean cut and glowing with health. And for the first time we were all performing, as Jim

McKay, ABC's voice of the Olympics, announced in his most excited announcer-ese, "Live and in color, via satellite to the whole world!"

Those four minutes changed my life. Before them I was a just another successful athlete. After them I was a famous face, everybody's girl next door, and an icon for a budding movement among women in sports. In my life off the ice, I would rely on the poise and discipline that I had learned on the ice, a discipline I had developed until it was part of me. After winning the gold, I tried to put a plan into effect for a career and a marriage, but my Long Program—with all its surprises—would be my partner in life, and we would both have adapt to each other.

None of that, however, was in my mind when my turn came to skate in the arena in France in 1968. I was a very focused young girl in a little chartreuse dress. Chartreuse, what a color! This past year, 1999, it has been very popular—a kind of *Jetsons*-retro fashionable color. But back in 1968 it was one of a kind, just like the one-of-a-kind woman who made it—my mom. She was a stage mom and a micromanager to beat the band. We were partners: I skated and she made the decisions—*all* the decisions. It would be that way until I became a mother and something changed in me. It wasn't until I had children of my own that I began to take back the parts of my life that I had always left to her: my career choices, my finances, and my choice of the coaches and producers and agents.

That short little chartreuse dress, with the simple rhinestone cuffs and the choker, was a pure Doris Fleming move. Mom found out that very near to Grenoble was the monastery where the monks made Chartreuse Liqueur. She thought that dressing me in chartreuse would send a subliminal message to the French people and that they would root for me, which in turn would help my confidence and endear me to the French fans.

Mom's idea was way too subtle (or just too far out) for the crowd, and I was too much in my own world to pay attention to her subtle gestures. An athlete, about to compete, has very little going on in her mind except for being totally focused, totally ready, totally in the moment. The world just stops. It seems to you that the whole planet is holding its breath, waiting for you to start, just you alone while the whole world waits: white ice, silver blades, and a mental road map to take you through three pieces of music, eighteen jumps, and five spins.

They call my name, and I skate onto the ice. The audience welcomes me. This is *my* moment. I'm way ahead on the compulsories, the school figures, and they count for sixty percent of your final score. So basically, I have already won the gold as long as I can make it through my four-minute program without a face plant, as skaters call an ungraceful fall on the ice.

Silence. I can hear the rustle of clothing and paper, a cough here and a sniffle there, as the crowd settles.

I am *terrified*, but I respond to fear as a challenge, the same way I use anger as a challenge—anger at my Mom, at my coach, at a competitor, at myself. Those emotions give me something immediate to conquer. My competitive nature comes forward. I will not let fear and anger beat me. I will win.

"Okay, be calm," I say to myself. "It's just another practice session like I've done ten thousand times before." The lush chords and relentless rhythm of Tchaikovsky's symphony

"*Pathetique*" pour out of the speakers. I hear the music as if it's an old friend, and I let it take me by the hand. I need an old friend like Tchaikovsky in a big way at this moment. As I go through my first toe loops I am tight and tentative. I get through all of the moves in the first section of my Long Program, but I feel like someone reciting the lyrics to a song and not like a singer giving life to the music.

Up I go for my double lutz to finish the first segment. I land unsurely, on two feet instead of one. Dick Button sees it in the announcer's booth, and no doubt the judges see it too.

"*Keep going, Peggy, Just get through it.*" I tell myself, but the fire and passion, the confidence and ease that I had the month before when I took home my fifth consecutive national championship, have all deserted me. All I have left is my training and my inner drive.

I am determined.

The languid and romantic theme of *Samson and Delilah* by Saint-Saëns fills the air, part two of my program. I start with a slow low spiral and move through toe turns and spin—nothing great, but not bad. I build to the three big moves at the end of the section: my second double axel of the program was supposed to be a spread eagle, double axel, spread eagle. The crowd doesn't know that I am going to try the double axel. As I approach my takeoff, I don't feel aligned. I scrap the double and do the single. "*At this stage of the competition,*" I think, "*better to try less and stay on my skates than risk a fall for points I don't necessarily need.*" I finish the movement with an outside spread eagle, an inside spread eagle, and a layback spin.

Pretty nice.

"*That's more like it. One more section and you're through it, Peggy!*"

Part three: Rossini's *La Gazza Ladra*. It is a piece he might as well have written for me—its joy, its hint of coquettishness, its exuberance are all emotions that I experience when my skating is really on. Even when it isn't, that music can lift me. I need that lift now. I'm still not flying on top of the music like I know I can be.

"Get through it, Peggy. Get through it! Winning when you don't have your best stuff is the real trick."

The end is in sight. The music crescendos. I step into a split jump double flip. That goes well. Then I go for another axel. Again it's fine, but still tentative. *"I'll make it up with an axel double salchow. I never mess those up."*

I take off on the axel. No problem, and then I open out on the salchow, which I never do. I do it this time and I don't complete the salchow. Nothing tragic, nothing that will lose me many points, but not my best. I still have one big move for my finish, a flying sit spin combination that feels just right.

It's over! My final Olympic performance. Did the nerves get to me? Did it look as clunky as I felt? I sit down to wait for the judges' scores. We don't have the "kiss and cry" area you see now on television, where the coach comes over and hugs the skater and gives her a big bouquet. I am isolated, sitting in what used to be the penalty box of a hockey rink, surrounded by glass. Carlo Fassi, my coach, can't get to me. Nobody can be around me until the marks flash up on the scoreboard.

So I sit there, not breathing hard yet straining to remain in total control. Up come the scores, and up soars my heart! I have won an Olympic gold—the only one America will win that year. I go and hug Carlo, and then I cry in my mom's arms.

I was lucky to win the Olympic gold medal when I did. I was also lucky that it was 1968. The story of the victory of a clean-cut American gave the country a break from the relentless Vietnam War and the assassinations of Martin Luther King and Bobby Kennedy. More significantly for me on a personal level, 1968 was the year that sports and the Olympics became big-time entertainment.

With satellites and color television—and a huge investment from ABC Sports—the Olympics had become a major media event: prime-time, just like Dick Van Dyke or *The Ed Sullivan Show*. This was part of the overall growth of TV sports. All those hours of sports programming that the networks had added needed personalities to appeal to the public. Arnold Palmer and then Jack Nicklaus benefited from that, and they became household words in golf. Billie Jean King and Chris Evert would, likewise become household names because of television. As the only American gold medal winner in 1968, I was a big story at exactly the moment at which the Olympics and skating first reached a mass audience. This wasn't true four years earlier for any Olympic athlete. I remember talking to my friend, Donna de Varona, who won two gold medals as a swimmer in 1964 in Tokyo. They didn't even make a videotape of her performance, but in 1968, only four years later, my video replay was everywhere.

For certain fortunate athletes, training, skill, and some other mysterious element come together and you rise to the top of your sport and stay there. Chris Evert had a run like that in tennis. So did Bjorn Borg, Arnold Palmer, Joe Montana—somehow, some way, these people found the secret. I was in that winning zone from 1964 to 1968. Blessed with a great coach, my own talent, and just as important, my determination, I went from success to sucess.

Early in 1968 ABC's *Wide World of Sports* selected me as Athlete of the Year for 1967, a major honor in the sports world. In those years it was the biggest award in sports. Muhammad Ali had received it when he was still Cassius Clay. Russian high jumper Valery Brumel, prescandal O.J. Simpson, race car legend Mario Andretti, and Olga Korbut were all winners. I was among the elite of the elite.

The ceremony was held in a beautiful chalet on Chamrousse, in Grenoble. The audience was filled with sports celebrities, corporate bigwigs, and a good-looking young actor named Robert Redford who was there doing research for the role that would establish him as a leading man in *Downhill Racer.*

Tom Moore, the president of ABC, gave a long speech about how fabulous I had been in my string of National and World championships. Then Roone Arledge, president of ABC Sports and the man who created the Olympics as a television event, lauded me to the skies. But I was still so new to the famous-athlete game that I had no idea what was expected of me when it came time to accept this great honor. They called my name, and I went up to the dais to get my award. I spoke into the mike.

"Thank you," I said.

The world's shortest acceptance speech. Then I went back to my seat.

The Academy Awards could use some acceptance speeches that length. After that, I learned to say a little more.

I was greatly honored to have won that award. It made me feel even more strongly that I *had* to win an Olympic gold medal. That was the missing piece.

I was born lucky. Winning the medal when I did and with the world the way it was was just another little bit of luck. When I was born I weighed 7 pounds 11 ounces and I was 21 inches long. Anyone who ever rolled dice or played a hand of blackjack can tell you those are lucky numbers.

I also think that as a woman and an athlete I chose the right sport at the right time. Figure skating was ready for change. When I first started to skate, it is fair to say, the sport was like gymnastics with some music in the background. You crammed a lot of moves into your program, which may or may not have had anything to do with your music. Carol Heiss, who won the Olympic gold medal in 1960 as well as five World titles, typified the sport at the time. She was a pretty girl, always very put together, and she could perform all the jumps and spins. She was athletic but not *too* athletic for a lady—remember, we are talking about a time when a "real lady" couldn't be too athletic. But times change and so do sports. Within a few years, I came to believe that skating could be more like art, if you could only find a way to put your whole self and your emotions into it and convey that to an audience. Skating is one of the few athletic endeavors in which taste and elegance and grace count in the standings.

A graceful baseball player like Joe DiMaggio, a lithe and acrobatic football player like Lynn Swann, a fluid basketball player like Michael Jordan—all of them were remarkable athletes. People will always remember them for the way they seemed to glide so effortlessly, moving under a fly ball, leaping for a reception, flowing like water between the outstretched arms of defenders. Their inherent grace and good taste made them memorable, but those qualities never showed up in the box score. Skating is the only sport that scores both by your athletic ability *and* your artistry.

That was lucky for me, because it so much embodied what I got out of skating and what I tried to put into it. Coming from a family that was always stressed because it was on thin ice financially, skating was the vessel into which I could pour my heart and soul. I was too shy to let that come out very much in my skating in my early years, but it's what made my skating different when the world in general and women in particular were looking for an athlete who skated to a different drummer. I don't mean to imply that in 1968 I was there to kick off the feminist movement, but the feelings of femininity that I was just learning about and trying to incorporate in skating were the same feelings that millions of woman were beginning to express more fully and openly in art, music, politics, marriage—in other words, in life. We wanted to be achievers, but being an achiever didn't mean that you stopped being a woman.

I am happy and proud to have been, in my own small way, part of that change. My eyes were first opened wide to the possibilities of growth and change in skating when I saw Donald Jackson, the great Canadian World Champion, land a triple lutz in competition on the first telecast of the World Championships in 1962. The triple lutz was a move that no one had tried under those circumstances before, but Don Jackson needed something major to win and he came right out and landed it at the very beginning of his program and he did it with confidence and authority. A few months later, when he came to perform for a press event at my practice rink, I was in a group of young skaters who saw him do the triple lutz in person. I felt like a teenybopper at a Beatles concert: I was positively in love with the guy. I wanted to do new things just like Don and wanted to do them with style and grace, just like Don.

It would be years, more than ten actually, before I would evolve the style that I felt truly expressed Peggy Fleming—a flowing pure line that had the feel of ballet and the spirit of a woman. I had always had that inclination within me, and seeing the great team of the Protopopovs had a great effect on me in 1964 when I was in my first Olympics (the one in which I came in sixth, which hardly anybody remembers). The way they moved, their choreography, their form—it all came out of the tradition of Russian ballet. I should add, right at the outset, that I am not a ballerina. People have credited me with bringing ballet into modern skating, or at least with popularizing it, and I am flattered. But what I brought was the spirit of ballet more than the techniques of dance. I loved the way that ballet united strength, agility, gracefulness, and emotion just as skating did.

I borrowed from ballet and from skaters like the Protopopovs and then, years later, from the irreplaceable John Curry. I had a major crush on John. Even though it never got beyond an emotional connection between us, it made me eager to learn. John and I would practice positions on the lawn in back of my house, using the sliding glass doors to check out our reflections, just the way ballet partners practice in front of a mirror. He had studied ballet quite seriously, and he taught me, among other things, how to hold my hands and spread my fingers to give myself a more graceful and longer line. Toller Cranston is another skater who has that ballet spirit. So did Janet Lynn and Dorothy Hamill. Katarina Witt has it to an extent—although that probably has more to do with the fact that she has the glamour and presence of a prima ballerina than the style of one.

It took years for me to get my skating to where I wanted to be. One of the reasons it took so long is that it was the antithesis of the kind of pretty-little-girl skating that my mom favored. There's a hard part to watching your young ones grow up and express themselves because, proud as you may be of their realizing their potential, you know that it is also the first step to your losing your control over them. My mom controlled me for many years. I think she knew that once the genie of true sensuality in my skating was released from the bottle I would become my own woman—and no longer her "little girl." It wasn't until I became a mother myself in 1977 that I felt that my skating and my life had broken free.

Compared to other girls growing up in the sixties, I wasn't really rebelling. I would never have had the opportunities I've had if Mom hadn't taken on the skating world with me. Mom was willing to absorb my terror before each competition and my natural shyness and somehow give them back to me in the form of confidence. The snide remarks from the more privileged kids, the self-serving criticism of the other coaches, the jostling and backbiting that goes on when you put a lot of ambitious, like-minded people together in a rink, all shooting for the same prize—those were all things that she confronted and dealt with. She was my shield.

Mom died in 1992. I often wonder what she would think of the sport today: the wild costumes, the sexy routines, the mugging for the audience. Athletically skaters are doing things now that we thought were impossible back then. I was astonished at Don Jackson's triple lutz, but now Michael

Weiss and Elvis Stojko land quadruple jumps regularly. When I look at videos of myself and compare them to Tara Lipinski, I am amazed at how much she can do and how well she does it. Only time will tell if her ability becomes art. On the other hand, her rival in 1998, Michelle Kwan, is a completely realized artist after my own heart. She has power, expression, artistry, and her own personal style. All great skaters have that personal style. John Curry had it, Robin Cousins has it. Brian Boitano has it. Lu Chen has it. It is something you never lose. You may slow down, lose a revolution or two on one of your moves, but if you have truly captured who you are in your skating (or, I suppose, in any other art) there will be no one exactly like you. That is what I always aspired to as a skater and, by extension, in my life as well.

My only regret as I look at the young skaters today is that I have had my glory days as a skater and they have it all still in front of them. On the other hand they have yet to find their partners in life, raise their families, build their homes . . . become who they are going to be after the Long Program on the ice is over and the Long Program of life moves on. It took a lot to get to this point and I am not sure I would want to do all of that again, but of one thing I am sure: I have been lucky through it all.

Whenever I am daunted by one of life's curve balls, I react as I used to do when I was scared to the pit of my stomach right before I competed. My life always returns to that moment on the ice: being scared, going into the spotlight, and then . . . away go the worries and I am just in the moment. There in that spotlight—whether the spotlight is the announcer's booth on ABC, the labor-and-delivery room at Good

Samaritan Hospital, a White House dinner, or the doctor's office at which I learn I have a fight with breast cancer on my hands—it is always the same for me.

I find a calm spot in the center of my soul.

I am gliding, moving free.

I feel as if I will never stop.

I push, floating on the music, always becoming something new.

1

Confidence

*I*f you had seen me in my early years, you would have had a hard time picking out the graceful skater that I worked very hard to become. If you first met me as an Olympic athlete or on a television special in a wispy costume gliding along ice as polished as a diamond, you probably think that I glide through life with my own personal symphony playing Mozart or Haydn, as I go to the supermarket or have the oil changed on my four-wheel drive.

Not quite.

The real me, the me before Peggy the Skater, was a scrawny, shy tomboy afraid to look in the mirror. It took many years for me even to recognize myself in the Peggy Fleming that the rest of the world sees. No matter how far any of us go in life, inside each of us is the kid we started out as.

If you had dropped into my fourth-grade class, you would have had a hard time picking out the future Olympic champion. In fact, you would have had a hard time picking me out at all. I was so shy that I usually scrunched myself into my chair in the back row hoping not to attract any attention at all. I was the kid who prayed the teacher never called on her, the one who *never* raised her hand.

I was desperately in need of confidence, especially in social situations. Like many other awkward children, it was only in the physical side of life that I began to find that confidence. Skating was the thing that eventually made everything else fall into place, but I was ready for skating when I discovered it only because I had spent years being physically active.

When I got outdoors, I felt free. When I got outdoors, I didn't mind attracting attention. If I were playing on the monkey bars, I would try the scariest, hardest tricks. It didn't matter that I had a permanent case of blisters on my hands or that my knees required a daily application of Band-Aids. That was the price I was willing to pay for showing off physically. The same thing was true when I began to play baseball. I was proud of how fast I ran the bases, how far I hit the ball, and how I could field and throw as well as the boys.

My mom and dad were both physically active, and they both loved the out-of-doors. Lucky for them: Fresh air and sunshine are free and abundant in California, and they couldn't have afforded much more. They always had to scramble to make ends meet, but I never knew about that. Kids rarely do.

My mom, Doris Deal, met my dad, Al Fleming, while she was waitressing at a restaurant in the Bay Area. The restaurant was a cutesy thing built inside a windmill. One afternoon she was serving a group of marines who were having a high old time. Among them was a powerfully built man with Irish good looks who had just been discharged from the corps.

My dad remembers that his eyes took in what my mom

would later refer to as her *"assets,"* and he told his buddies, "I am going to marry that girl." He did, and my three sisters and I are the results.

A lot has been written about how my mother shaped my career, but it was my dad who first got me into skating. He was not a simple man: He could be loving, full of high spirits, and always ready for a good time, but at other times his face could darken and he could get angry in a scary way. His background— a strict Catholic upbringing followed by marine corps training— tells the story of one side of his character: a lot of repression.

Having five women around our house was more than he knew how to handle. His response, when it wasn't just to have fun, was to be strict. For example, when we were teenagers just starting to think about looking womanly, he was totally against makeup or even a hint of glamour in his daughters. I would spend hours putting on makeup that I thought would look discreet enough that Dad would never notice. But I would make it only to the bottom of the stairs and Dad would take one look and send me back up to the bathroom to take it off. Of course, I'd stash all my makeup in my bag, and on the way to whatever party I was going to, I'd put lipstick and eye-liner on in the car. As my husband, Greg, will be the first to tell you, the big difference in me as a grownup is that now I *openly* put my makeup on in the bathroom, then I still work on it in the car.

The war experience marked my dad, which affected all of us in the family. A Japanese grenade landed on his tank and killed most of his friends. It smashed his leg up and he had to have a metal plate put in. He also came down with malaria, and I remember his screams when the fever came on strong. Mom would close the door so we wouldn't hear, but closing doors in houses rarely accomplishes much: Everybody knows what's going on.

My dad's way of dealing with this was to be as happy-go-lucky as possible—with plenty of help from his buddies and the bottle. Drinking was also an occupational hazard in his line of work: He was a pressman in the newspaper business. You see, you'd run a loud press all day and you'd pretty much need to blow off steam at the end of the shift with your friends. You'd drink and you'd smoke, and my dad did both— which is probably why he had three heart attacks before his final and fatal one at the age of forty one.

But in the beginning he and Mom were two young lovers starting out life in the golden sun of California. They built themselves a family pretty rapidly. First, my sister Janice was born in 1947, and then I came along in '48. They named me Peggy partly because the doctor in the labor and delivery room was singing "Peg O' My Heart" during my mom's labor. After me, Maxine showed up in '51 and Cathy in '54. Cathy was born on my birthday, and I always said I didn't get a party for my birthday, I got a sister instead.

They didn't have hippies then, but in a way my folks were early hippies. My mom quit college, to the great disapproval of her mother. In 1946, Doris and Al Fleming bought ten acres of land in Morgan Hill and built our house with their own hands. Dad had a job then at the *San Jose Mercury News,* one of many jobs that he would hold as we moved from town to town and from home to home. I am so glad that I have those early memories of that little farm. Those memories are a safe haven that I can return to in my mind when I need to put my life in perspective.

We had chickens on the farm as well as cows and horses,

including an old mare and a young stallion that hadn't been broken when we got him. We used to ride the mare, sometimes two girls at a time, and I thought Dad was a real swashbuckler when he broke that stallion all by himself. We had a pig too, which I thought of as mine.

Maybe you can look into this portrait of a childhood and see the outlines of my Olympic future, but when I remember those days—especially the pig—I see Peggy Fleming, future spokeswoman for the National Pork Producers Council (one of the jobs I would hold later in my career as an endorser and a star of commercials).

I loved that pig, but, our Doberman pinscher, whom I also loved, didn't.

One afternoon, for no apparent reason other than the basic nature of Dobermans, he jumped the barnyard fence and killed the pig. I cried as much as a little girl can cry, but that was just the beginning. Mom and Dad were afraid that the Doberman had become a danger; if it could attack the pig, it might attack one of us. Dad took his gun, went way out into a field so we wouldn't hear or see, and shot the dog. Not only had I lost my pet pig but we lost the family dog, too.

I didn't pine for too long. Mom and Dad liked sports and games as much as I did, or at least they pretended that they did, and they encouraged my sisters and me to go outside and enjoy ourselves. We were so into games that I remember the summer flying by one year in the late fifties. We were low on funds and the Fleming sisters camped by a lake with my mom while Dad went back to the Midwest to look for work.

We were kind of gypsies in that summer. My sisters and I spent the whole summer running, jumping, tree climbing, rope skipping, and singing around the campfire. These things seemed to be the perfect thing to do, and I enjoyed doing them with my family. I enjoyed doing them with my friends. I guess I just enjoyed being a tomboy, but they don't give out Olympic gold medals for being a tomboy.

One Saturday afternoon in December 1957, my mom saw an ad in the paper for a newly opened skating rink in the Bay Area that was offering a special introductory bargain price. I was nine years old, and my dad loved skating—in mom's words, he was "a nut on the subject." When my folks were courting, he had even taken a job setting up bowling pins to earn extra cash to go skating. So when Mom showed Dad the ad, he packed us all in the car and I was on the way to the thing that would make a new me.

It was like that scene in *City Slickers* where Billy Crystal, who has just turned forty and has gone on a cattle drive out West to resolve his mid-life crisis, asks the Jack Palance character, Curly, what the secret to life is. Curly holds up his index finger, saying the secret is "one": All you have to do is find one thing that you love.

I had my "one" moment at the age of nine. From that day on, I was a different girl. I had found the thing that made everything else fall into place.

The little girl who liked to show off on the monkey bars finally had something beyond a playground game to excel at. That was it, I finally had a *craft*, an art, a calling. Not that after an hour flopping on the ice with my father I was able to see the plan for the rest of my life, but something deep inside me knew. I had discovered something that I loved, something that gave me great pleasure, something that made me feel free, and— this was a first!—something that made me feel pretty.

Pretty was not the word that came to mind when I looked at myself in the mirror. I had the little-girl silhouette of a string bean in a dry summer, and my hair was thin and scraggly. But when I started skating, I could feel prettier by the way I moved, by my posture, by the position of my arms and legs, even by the tilt of my head. But before I felt pretty, I had to feel free and in control—that was the door that skating first opened. After that first time with my dad, I wanted to skate again . . . and again . . . and again. Being good at something—and having that something be a thing I loved to do—worked a change in me.

The timid tomboy who never cared how she looked finally started to blossom. For the first time I had a feeling of confidence, something I had never known before. It is something I have since come to believe in to the core of my soul: Confidence is the first and most important building block in becoming a fulfilled person. Confidence enables you to believe "I can do something that will make other people admire me. I can make my body stronger. I can compete and, if I don't win, I believe I have it in me to work harder and win the next time."

I was born a competitor. I always wanted to be best, not just better than the few girls who enjoyed sports the way I did, but better than the boys as well. It was a source of great pride to me when, years later, at a Little League game, I retrieved a foul ball and zipped it over to the first-base coach. "Wow, Mom," my son said with pride, "you don't throw like a girl." I was proud too—although if *anyone* but my son made such a patronizing remark, I wouldn't feel quite so warm and proud about it.

I began to realize that if I could make things into a game, I wanted to win. Even in math class, back in the third grade, I recall only getting interested when my teacher turned the math assignment into a game. That was all I needed to hear. I had never given a hoot about math and my grades showed it, but after that I absolutely had to win that competition.

That will to win didn't leave me when I grew up. One of my first paychecks was for appearing in my first NBC special, "Here's Peggy Fleming." It was for $35,000—which was a dazzling amount of money when you think that in his best year my dad probably brought home $10,000. Like the good red-blooded American girl that I was, I took that paycheck and used part of it to buy a fast car, not just any fast car, but a Porsche, a maroon Porsche. It was a real kick driving it, but the thing about fast cars is you never really get to see what they can do under normal driving conditions. Why spend all that money on a great machine just to look cool?

Our neighbors, the Melis, were members of the local Porsche club, and they invited us to come to an event one afternoon. Barbara Meli, who enjoyed speed the way I did, was the Ladies Champion race driver in our division. She asked me to join her for the race. We strapped ourselves in, put on our helmets, and she hit the accelerator. "This is terrific," I said.

"Want to give it a try?"

"Why not?"

I got in the driver's seat of our Porsche and drove the track. You get one test lap and then the last two are timed. All by myself in the car, I had the same sense that I used to feel when I was doing school figures in skating. On a racecourse, as on the ice, if you want to win, you have to follow the course exactly. As I drove the course, I could feel the adrenaline kick in. I was having fun, so much fun in fact that I won and became the Ladies Champion on that first day. I even beat my husband, Greg. Yeah!

All through my life, understanding the rules of the game

made me want to win. That was certainly the case when I was the most determined nine-year-old on ice in the whole state of California.

Every time I stepped onto the ice, it was important that I was the best one out there. People who know something about my life know the enormous role that my mother played in making me a champion. In the beginning Dad was there too, stoking the competitive fires. The same streak of toughness that made him such a strict disciplinarian showed itself in his determination to get me started in skating and to back me as far as my competitive drive would take me.

We moved to Pasadena when I was eleven, and I became friendly with another young girl, Susie Berens, who was into skating as much as I was. Years later we would skate in the ice shows, and when both of us had our young children on tour with us, we would share the same baby-sitter. Our parents arranged it so that we could practice from five to seven each morning, when we could have the ice all to ourselves. The only problem was that the ice wasn't in very good shape, still rough from the public session the night before with a few hours of late-night speed skating practice thrown in. The speed skaters left a smooth ring on the outside but the rest of the ice was all dinged up from the public free-for-all.

My dad was on the night shift at that time, working to get out the morning edition of the paper. One morning, after watching my frustration with the crummy ice surface, he said, "If they would teach me how to run the Zamboni"—the big machine they use to make the surface smooth—"I could make the ice ready for you and Susie."

Dad had to be there anyway, so it gave him something to do. We would arrive at the arena in pitch-blackness, and Dad would make his way across the building to the light switch. It was big and empty, dark and scary in there for the first few moments, waiting alone until Dad turned on the lights. He would resurface the ice and I would start skating on the first ice of the day.

Here's where the competition part comes in. I figured that if we got to the rink fifteen minutes earlier, I would get that much more time ahead of Susie. "That'll really get her," I thought, and it did. But Susie was also competitive. She started showing up earlier, which only made me come earlier still. Eventually we reached a point where it was ridiculously early, so we both started showing up at five again. It was important to me, even for a little while, to find a competitive edge.

I liked being first and still do.

Even if it meant getting up at an ungodly hour, skating was magic to me. Our family was financially and emotionally stressed all the time, like many families. Skating took me away from that and gave me a way to focus away from my family's problems onto me, on gliding and feeling free. There was nothing I could have loved more.

While I was having the time of my life, my mother was getting a different but no less deep satisfaction out of it. Part of the reason, of course, was what any mother would feel: "If it brings out something good in my daughter and helps her develop, then I want her to do it and I will do whatever I need to do."

But human beings are never that uncomplicated. My mother was somebody's daughter too, and by helping me to reach a dream—a dream that, frankly, I didn't even know I had at the beginning—she was also letting *her mother* live out the dreams that she had once had for my mom, her daughter.

I wouldn't have started skating if it weren't for my Dad, but

I became a *skater* because of my mom. It is not stretching the point to say, "We became a skater," two people, one pair of skates. We each had a job to do to make me a champion skater, and I certainly didn't do it on my own. Hardly anybody achieves great things completely solo, even in the solitary sport of skating. I had my personal reasons for working hard, not the least of which was that skating made me feel special. My mom had reasons that were no less compelling and strong. These days television commentators always seem to talk about Olympic athletes "pursuing their dreams," and it's true—you don't get to the top of the medal stand without powerful dreams. But I didn't start out with something as big as an Olympic dream. My mom had a whole lot of big dreams she had never lived out for her mother.

My grandma, Erma May Deal, was a proper lady, always completely put together. Her hair was always done, her make-up always perfectly applied, her clothes always spiffy and coordinated. I get my concern with appearance from her and from Grandpa, too. I remember countless winter mornings, getting up to go to practice, and there was my grandpa in the kitchen already in his suit and tie. I would tease him about it. "Grandpa, all dressed up and nowhere to go? Why bother, when there's no one to impress?" He would tell me that he wasn't out to impress anyone. Feeling put together made him sit straighter, feel better and present himself better for the day. It made him confident.

Grandma was a woman of two eras. She was a very religious person in the old-fashioned way that strong Baptists are. She played the piano, sang with the family in the parlor, and played endless religious programs on the radio. But she had also been a bit of a groundbreaker, having packed up and left home on her own to go to college, which was a big deal for women in that day. She was someone who always gave the impression that she held herself to very high personal standards.

Those standards explain how she ended up in California. She was the daughter of a judge in Missouri, where she attended college. When she was a young woman, her mother died. Almost immediately, her father married her mother's younger sister. Obviously something strange had happened, something that she thought was horrible, something she never, *ever* talked about. She picked up and left for California by herself and never came back. On that train ride she met Grandpa, who was a young soldier, the son of a farmer, on his way to the First World War.

Grandma Erma had high hopes for her daughter, but my mom, who was the strongest willed person I have ever met, didn't follow the script. For one thing, my mom was physically the opposite of grandma. Where grandma was slim and ultra-feminine, my mom was a big-boned woman. Instead of indulging in grandma's girlish pastimes at the piano and dressing up, Mom was out playing with her four older brothers: surfing, playing tennis, hiking, swimming, rock climbing. It's not hard to see where I got my tomboy genes from . . . as well as my cheekbones. Mom had beautiful and delicate high cheekbones, and they made her a very striking woman. Erma May believed that those cheekbones would bring out the inner Katharine Hepburn in my mom, and Grandma enrolled Mom in ballet classes, tap classes, and singing lessons. Unfortunately, those were not things my mother excelled at. My mom was good in school and one heck of a writer, and she followed her mother's lead by going to college. "Maybe she isn't going to be the belle of the ball," Grandma thought, "but she is going to be a career woman."

When I started skating and wearing pretty costumes, paying attention to my looks, and moving beautifully to the kind of music that Grandma loved, my mother took great satisfaction in finally giving her mom the daughter she had always wanted. I felt the tremendous emotional power and I drew strength from it.

I enjoyed it—I wasn't a little wind-up skating doll that my mom and my grandma exploited in order to play out their own unfulfilled dreams. But when you add my instant love affair with skating to my mother's natural instinct to help her daughter shed her shy self and take on the world and my grandmother's wish for an artistic and accomplished next generation, you have three determined women working toward one goal.

Three strong women working toward one thing is always a very powerful force.

With my family behind me, I was never alone out on the ice, which was a good thing because the world of ice skating back then was different than it is today. Serious ice skating was something that only well-off kids did. Lessons added up pretty quickly to a small fortune. Costumes did too. To put it into some perspective, it cost more for a one-hour lesson than my dad could earn in that same hour running the *Mercury News* presses. If I had thought I didn't fit in as the mousy little kid in the back row of fourth grade, I was really a fish out of water among all the affluent little girls doing their spins and jumps at the skating rink.

I was in my own world, and I didn't notice. I had found something that made me feel whole. I was lucky to make this discovery when I was nine years old. Some people go a whole lifetime before they discover it—whether it's fly-fishing, golf, cooking, or growing tomatoes. You know it when you find it: It's the thing that makes time pass differently so that you give all your hours to it and it still doesn't feel like too much.

Part of the reason I fell in love with skating and blossomed was I had a natural gift. Make that two natural gifts: an aptitude for skating and a deep (and largely untapped) reservoir of determination.

People often talk about how being a trained athlete requires a sense of goals, focus, and discipline. I think that makes the inner game sound a lot harder and more rigid than it really is. The first thing an athlete requires is joy. I loved skating. Not that I loved getting up at five in the morning, getting to the rink before school, going to school all day until heading back to the rink after school, staying there until just before dinner, then doing homework, before flopping into bed. It's just that I loved skating so much I was willing to pay the price. It must have offered something to my mom and dad as well. They were the ones who took me to the rink, sat in the stands, and paid for the lessons.

I was grateful then, and remain grateful, but I was also glad to get out of the house. Our unsettled finances led to our perpetually picking up and moving to new houses and new towns as Dad sought work. My dad's temper and uptightness around his daughters and my mom's uptightness around my dad—these were all stresses that weighed on me. We were not an unhappy family, but we weren't the world's most stable one either. So while I often felt lost in the crowd at home, at the rink I felt that I had all the room in the world.

I wanted more of that freedom in my life, and I was bound and determined to work as hard as I could to make that happen.

2

Coaches: My School Days on Ice

In my first year on the ice, I skated nearly every day, one or two hours a day. Mom and Dad were happy to see me doing something that I was really good at, something at which I had some success. When I competed in local events, I wasn't finishing in sixth or seventh . . . I was winning, or at least coming close. My folks could see that I was taking skating seriously and getting better and that I had the desire. But even desire, parental support, and talent can't grow in a vacuum. I needed teachers and mentors. More important, I needed that one teacher who, like a gifted sculptor, could take the formless clay of a young skater and shape it into the figure of a champion. It took a while, but we got there.

It started with a trip to the Midwest when I was ten. Dad and Mom packed up the car and we went East for six months while my father learned to operate a color press. It was a big change for the Fleming sisters of California. Summer heat and humidity, winter cold and snow—these were new experiences. At least I had my skating to give me some continuity.

Mom, who always had an instinct for finding the right teacher for me, took me to meet Harriet Lapish, a sweet lady who looked like the average American mom. Harriet had me take a series of skating tests, and when I scored well, she advised that I get into competition. I liked Harriet and the way she went out of her way to get the most out of our few months together. I wouldn't say I learned that much, but I began to understand how to work with a coach and get the most out it. Whenever I was feeling a little lazy—which all kids feel sometimes—my mom would get on my case. So while I was beginning to learn skating, I was learning something else too, something that would carry me all through my competition years—how to get Peggy Fleming to give one hundred percent. Mom would motivate me by encouragement, by scolding, by confrontation, and by guilting me out. Whatever it took, Doris Fleming did it.

I sometimes think of the effect on my three sisters of all this attention paid to one daughter. I didn't notice anything then—they were as supportive of me as my mom was—but seen from the vantage-point now of a grown woman and mother of two, I know that my sisters paid a price, and I'm sorry for it. Back then all I knew was that I liked to skate and my family liked having me skate, so it all seemed perfectly natural.

When we moved back to California, my mom went to see Gene Turner, a skating teacher who had been recommended by Harriet. Gene had once been a skating partner of Sonja Henie, and he was the Men's National Champion in 1940–41. At our first meeting I was impressed with what a distinguished guy he was—so put together. He always wore a suit and had a dignified air about him, and he was handsome to boot. It was a mixture that commanded respect.

When he asked me to skate, I was a little in awe, but I did as I was told. Perhaps it was the respect he inspired, but Gene later said that he could see that in addition to having some talent, I also struck him as obedient and disciplined.

Those few laps around the ice were a defining moment in my life. When I finished them, I had my first big-time coach. He was an inspiring man with his own unusual, yet effective, teaching methods.

One of the things that made Gene a good coach was the way he could inject fun into things that could have become boring and routine. He would make up games: for example, who could do the most jumps in a row without falling or making a mistake. Or he had us draw poker chips from a hat to determine our next routine—if you drew red you would do a solo, white meant a pairs number, blue meant a trio.

On Saturdays, we would have the ice all to ourselves from six to eight in the morning. Gene would stand with his microphone and shout instructions. He was also big on school figures. Sometimes he would turn the lights out and have us do our figure-eights and circles in the dark. At first I thought it was crazy, but then I began to see the point: There we were in a skating rink in January in pitch-blackness, doing figures without being able to see what we were doing. He wanted us to *feel* what we were doing, and he succeeded. I developed an inner sense of where the circle was, and learned an important lesson: Concentrating on technique will take you just so far. There comes a point where you need to feel what you are doing without thinking or looking down at the ice.

After a few months, Gene thought I had progressed enough

to enter a competition. My first competition was held at the Sutro Baths, an old family resort and amusement park on the ocean cliffs in San Francisco. When my mom was young, it was quite the place for a family outing. They used to have different swimming pools—hot and cold, salt and freshwater, and you could spend your day going from pool to pool. The pools were all closed down years before I got there, but you could still see where they had been. It was gorgeous even when you went into the rest rooms; You could look out through the windows at the waves crashing on the rocks below. You walked down a thousand steps—or at least it seemed that many—to the skating rink.

The event was the Bay Area Juvenile competition. I didn't really know much about competition so I just went out there and did my routine. I still have a video from those days, actually from a month or two later. I remember feeling so graceful and beautiful at the time, but I look at the video now and I can't see why I felt that way. I seem so coltish jumping without any apparent sense of the music. Nevertheless, the judges at Sutro must have seen something in my effort, because they gave me first place.

Two weeks later I entered the Pacific Coast Championship in Los Angeles. I still didn't understand how hard competition could be and how much attention it demanded, so I wasn't the least bit nervous. I stayed loose, went out there and skated, and didn't even feel a trace of jitters in my stomach.

As soon as I got off the ice, I headed straight for the coffee shop and the pastries. When the judges gave my marks, Gene ran in to get me and dragged me out to see.

"What are they doing? " I asked.

"Those are your marks," Gene said.

"Oh," I said without a trace of interest as they posted my losing scores: dead last in the school figures! I didn't even qualify to do my free skating. The judges had seen enough.

I was humiliated, especially for my family, who had made the drive down to L.A. The sheer embarrassment of it all gave me a jolt. From that day on I was serious about every competition I entered.

My next big competition was at Squaw Valley, just before the 1960 Olympic Winter Games. It also happened to be the same Pacific Coast Championships in which I had embarrassed myself the year before. It was also the first time I skated in the winter cold. I had learned something from my loss in L.A.: I had learned how to be nervous. This time I was such a ball of nerves that even my mom couldn't shake me out of it. It was a stroke of pure luck, that they had me skating first. Instead of getting into a stew watching the other girls, I went out there and skated for all I was worth.

This time I didn't come in last. I won.

And so I continued skating and skating . . . four, sometimes five hours a day. At this point my mom began to sense that I could go far as a skater. As would happen for many years to come, she made the decisions and I skated. I hardly looked up to see what was going on around me. If Mom wanted me to work with a new coach, then that's what I did. That was how I went from Gene Turner to Tim Brown. One day I was doing what Gene told me to do, and the next day it was Tim. I did what they told me to do with as much energy and concentration as I could muster, and at that age it was a considerable amount.

I started working with Tim when I was eleven. Where Gene was emotional and artistic, Tim was more intellectual. After every lesson, he would insist that I write down what I had learned. He wanted to see what I took from the lesson: my progress as well as my mistakes and my analysis of them. Tim would even correct my spelling! It kind of makes sense for a guy who was so into technique and school figures. Although I thought it was an immense pain back then, I now realize that the act of writing something down makes an indelible mark in your brain. I actually wrote and drew out the designs of all of my moves, which is a technique I still use to this day in analyzing skaters on ABC.

In 1960 we moved to Pasadena, which meant a new coach for me. I am not sure if we moved because Dad had already found work there with the *L.A. Times* or if Dad looked for work there so that I would have the opportunity to work with Bill Kipp, who was a hot up-and-coming coach.

Bill was another one in a long string of handsome male coaches. I have always responded best to male coaches, and I would work a little harder to please them. Sometimes it was because I felt a little attraction to them. It never developed into anything romantic, but there was a kind of electricity that helped my skating.

If things had developed according to the script, I would have stayed with Bill for a number of years and taken my place alongside his pupils, who were among the top U.S. hopefuls. But on Valentine's Day, 1961, Sabena Airlines flight number 548 took off from Idlewild Airport in New York City (now JFK) en route to Brussels, the first stop on the way to the World Championships that were about to begin in Prague.

After an overnight flight that seemed normal and uneventful, the plane lost power and crashed into a field outside Brussels killing all eighteen members of the U.S. team, along with coaches, officials, and family members. Among those family members was the great Maribel Vinson Owen, mother of Laurence Owen, one of the top U.S. prospects. Maribel herself had been a six-time U.S. champion and an Olympic silver medalist, as well as the first woman reporter for *The New York Times* sports section. Both she and her daughter were killed in the crash. Bill Kipp was also among those lost. A missing generation of skaters left a big empty space on the ice for the younger athletes, and I was among them. Looking back on it, that tragedy was a huge event in my life, but at the time I don't remember thinking of it that way. I was sad, but I continued to skate. No matter what, I kept on skating.

With the death of the team, the skating world was in disarray, and with the loss of Bill Kipp, I needed a new coach. Word must have been getting around that I was a good young prospect because a few coaches approached Mom before we settled on Doryann Swett, a colleague of Bill Kipp's. Doryann took me to Montana for the Pacific Coast Competition, where I really aced my school figures and sailed through my free skate even though I had come down with the flu. When I was done, I felt really sick and threw up right there on the ice. Thankfully, the judges didn't grade me on my after-skating decorum. Winning in the Pacific Coast Novice division meant I could go on to Boston for the Nationals.

That's when Doryann made a mistake.

As the daughter of a man who was paid by the hour (and not very much at that), I had a different background than most of the other young skaters. By and large, they came from much more affluent families, they had beautiful costumes made for them, and their moms had professional hairdos and wore expensive clothes. Not me and not my mom. We made all my costumes at home. We would look through patterns and catalogues, and

Mom and I would cut and sew fabric and paste on sequins until we had something that looked like a skating costume. It always had to be a very chaste and proper skating costume. Those were the days when women skaters, even the top stars, skated in what we called "sensible underpants" nothing high-cut to make the leg look longer. Sensible underpants were unrevealing and only a step above boxer shorts.

So I skated in homemade costumes, and my mom stood out from the other skating moms by being the one with the plain hairdo, no makeup, and an unexciting wardrobe. Although I never heard it directly, we were often made to feel that we were crashing the party. We just weren't from the same world as the more well-off families whose sons and daughters were part of the country club set known as "the skating world."

Doryann was part of that skating world and it proved to be the undoing of our relationship. Right after the competition in Montana, she took my mom aside and basically gave her an ultimatum: "Either you get a new wardrobe and hairstyle or I don't go to Boston with you."

Guess who didn't go to Boston? As my mom later put it, "I couldn't even afford to have one costume made for Peggy. How was I supposed to buy new clothes for myself? I realized then Doryann has grasped Peggy's star potential and she was beginning to see herself as far more than a coach. She wanted to share the limelight as Peggy's mentor, spokesperson, role model, manager, best friend, and confidante. In short, she wanted to take my place. Exit Doryann."

I went to Boston without her and came in second in the Nationals.

I was developing a new style and the world was beginning to notice. People have often said my skating is like ballet, and in certain ways it is. In the next phase of my training, Mom continued to pick coaches the way some people keep looking for a new and better car. John Nicks followed Doryann Swett, and we worked together for a year. Then came Peter Betts, the coach who worked with me on the routine that first brought me to national attention. A former ice dancer, he was really into ballet and body line and stretching—all things that became part of my skating.

The big change in my style, though, came about through Bob Turk. He was a choreographer, but not a skater, or at least not much of a skater, but he understood enough to translate the spirit of ballet to the ice. Mom felt this was just what I needed to put a little more creativity and self-expression into the exhibition numbers I was beginning to get requests for, now that I was becoming a presence on the skating scene.

Bob came from the dance world. He had choreographed numbers for the Ice Capades and the Lido review in Paris. I am not sure my Mom knew what that meant. Probably the Paris part impressed her, but neither of my parents would have been too happy if they knew that the Lido was a live, topless review. When I found out, I kept it to myself.

Bob became my ballet-on-ice mentor with the emphasis on the ice part. On the dance floor, when you land, the move is essentially over. On ice, you just keep moving. Every move extends and creates its own line. Skating has a much more flowing aspect. Great ballet gives the illusion of gliding, flow-ing motion. With skating it comes with the territory. It seemed to me and to Bob that this was a great and basically untapped new frontier in skating—the ability to flow with the music in an expressive and continuous way.

All the inner turmoil of adolescence—anybody's adolescence—needs channeling. Bob understood that putting expression into my skating was helping me pour my soul into something that would hold it and let it grow.

Today, as I look at the tapes of my early work with Bob in the competition that led to the Junior Ladies Nationals in Long Beach, I think I look more like a bumper car than a ballerina. But in my fourteen-year-old mind, I was a gliding and graceful ice princess. I felt pretty so I skated that way and took third place, which qualified me for my first Senior Nationals the next year in Cleveland.

My parents and I stayed in a cheap motel, the kind where someone flushing in room #1 can wake up everyone down to room #20. But it was all we could afford, and the excitement of being there more than made up for the low-rent accommodations.

Cleveland was the place where just a few years before, Harriet Lapish had first seen some promise in my skating. I was back again, still a young girl, but now I was competing with the best in the country in an event that would determine not only the ladies championship, but also the Olympic team.

I was in no way prepared for what followed.

I won first place! On that day I was, in the opinion of the judges, the best woman skater in America, which meant I was chosen to represent America in the 1964 Olympic Winter Games in Innsbruck, Austria.

I was even less prepared for a trip to Austria. When we left California, we had only packed for a week. I didn't even have a warm coat, but Mom and I were off to the Olympics by way of New York, where the U.S. team gathered to prepare. You could tell that the United States Olympic Committee was as surprised as I was at my being there. They didn't even have rooms for Mom and me, so we stayed at the YWCA on 51st Street. My mom felt snubbed and she really laid into the Olympic Committee, who ended up apologizing for what they called "an unfortunate oversight." We ended up at the Barbizon, which was the hotel of choice for young debutantes.

Those first few days, we skated at the New York Skating Club in Manhattan, and my mom struck up a conversation with Mrs. Phyllis Kennedy, who was a friend of my coach, Peter Betts. Mom mentioned that she needed to work on my costumes, and she asked Mrs. Kennedy if she had a sewing machine. "Yes," Mrs. Kennedy replied, "would you like to come to our place and use it?"

Mom accepted the invitation.

It turned out that Mrs. Kennedy had a sewing machine, *and* a mansion, *and* a nearby skating rink in Oyster Bay, an exclusive and very pretty old suburb on the north shore of Long Island. We stayed there for a week, and I loved having such a quiet and beautiful environment to train in. The outdoor rink got me used to the outdoor cold in Innsbruck. Mrs. Kennedy sensed what kind of shape we were in financially and offered me a warm coat and some sweaters that had belonged to her daughter.

I was ready for my first trip outside of America and my first Olympic Games.

It's strange the way we remember things. There was so much that was completely new and different for me at Innsbruck, the site of the Winter Olympic Games. But the thing I remember most was not the pine forests, not the crisp clean Alpine air— but that the smell was different. Even the cars and trucks smelled different. I think it was the fuel they used.

Then we arrived at the Olympic Village. To be around so many young, eager, athletic, and focused kids—kids like myself who spent all those thousands of hours practicing their lessons—I was in a new world.

I was also away from Mom for the first time, although the Olympic Committee found her a room in town. If Mom could have stayed in the village, I am pretty sure she would have. She was as worried about how I would do on my own as she was about the competition. Would I remember to wake up on time? Would I remember my gloves? My skates? And what about leaving me to my wits and good upbringing in what amounted to a small town full of exuberant, good-looking, very physical teenagers . . . most of them boys?

Mom didn't have to worry about any of that. Boys were the furthest thing from my mind, although I did like going to the little disco they had set up for the athletes. There was even this one skater I had a mini-crush on. We danced a few times, but that was the extent of it.

I was proud to be on the team, but I hated the Olympic uniforms. Even then, fashion was becoming an important part of the total package. How you looked said a lot about your style, and your style was what made your skating different and special. Those tight ski pants and geeky wool jackets with red and blue stripes on the collar were not my style. Still, when all the American team walked into the arena with all the thousands of other athletes, all of us in our uniforms and all of us marching behind our flags—it was breathtaking: a hundred thousand people roaring and applauding, under the snow-capped Alps and, the bluest blue sky in the world. Everybody should have a first Olympics—it moves you, takes over your emotions and overwhelms you until you can hardly think. And everyone should be fortunate enough to go on to have a second Olympics, so that you have time to take it in.

I remember the practice sessions as well as the actual competition. I loved skating on the speed skating oval next to the indoor rink, but the cold winter sunshine was blinding. I was glad I had my outdoor tune-up in Oyster Bay.

Seeing the other skaters in Innsbruck was a very important thing for my growth as an athlete and a competitor. Being there gave me a different perspective on the European skaters. This was before the days of skating on television, so I really had no idea what the competition looked like or what their style was.

I was very respectful of what the other women did athletically, but not esthetically. Oh, brother! The gold-medal winner, Sjoukje Dijkstra of the Netherlands, was a huge, muscular lady who performed huge jumps. All I could think was, "Couldn't she be a little more feminine?" Seeing what I didn't want to be made me resolve to be both athletic *and* feminine. I could begin to see the skater I wanted to be. Once you have a picture like that in your mind, your goal has more clarity. You know where you want to be.

Style wasn't my only goal. Technique was still something I had to master. I was happy with my Olympic performance and placed sixth. To be number six in the whole world at age fifteen isn't so bad, but if I had been better at school figures—which counted for sixty percent of your score back then—I would have placed higher. School figures have now been replaced by two programs (the Short and the Free Skate) that determine the winner. There is more style and art to the sport these days, but the school figures instilled focus and discipline.

Let me explain a little bit further about school figures. If you've never had to do them, probably your only experience of them is seeing some videotape of skaters moving very, very slowly while a bunch of judges and spectators stare at their feet.

Modern competitive skating actually began with school figures, which is why it counted for so much of the program. When I was competing in the Olympics you had to perform six different school figures. There were dozens of figures that we had to have in our repertoire, but each year, competitors had to demonstrate mastery of six of them. You knew at the beginning of the year what those figures would be but only in the week before the competition did you learn which foot you would start on.

A week before you competed, the judges or skating federation would tell you which foot you were required to perform on and what figure. At my second Olympics, we were assigned the most difficult loop for me, the Left Forward Paragraph Loop. I really hated that figure. Worse, we all had to do it on the left foot, which isn't my best one. I was terrified, but I got through it.

There were a few theories regarding my early weakness in school figures. For one thing, I wasn't a noisy skater. Even though the grinding sound of blades on the ice may tell some skaters when they are not skating a figure correctly, I hated the sound. I wanted to skate silently and beautifully. Grinding is not the sound you make when your skating is light, not the sound of a sure skater. A quiet skater is confident on her blades, doing the things that are comfortable for her. When my skating was silent, I was doing things the way I wanted them. So silence, in my case, was golden, but some thought it didn't help my figures.

I thought the main reason had more to do with where I skated rather than how. At the rink in Pasadena, we skated on hockey ice, which is as white as can be so that the painted lines are very visible to the players. This is not what you want for figures. When you skate a figure on clean gray ice—say a Right Forward Outside Rocker, which is three circles in a line—each skater rents his or her own little patch of ice so you can look down and actually see the pattern your skates make on the ice. You do a figure over and over again, moving a few inches at a time so that each figure is more or less on virgin ice. That way you can see your progress and where you still need work. My patch on the Pasadena hockey ice was always so white, even first thing in the morning, that it was hard to see my figures.

I knew that my own personal Long Program—my plan for my life as a skater—required more work on school figures. There was a coach in Colorado named Carlo Fassi, who was well known for his work on this very technical and necessary aspect of competition. Before I made that move, however, I met—or should I say Mom brought me to meet—another coach whom I have continued to work with until this day. While I can say that Carlo Fassi made me an Olympic champion, another coach, Bob Paul, had an equal role in making me Peggy Fleming. Carlo was the substance, but Bob the style.

Bob and I joined forces after the 1964 Olympics. Mom had gone coach shopping again, and she was determined that I would compete at the next Winter Games in Grenoble. She was even more determined that I would win. She wasn't happy with many of the coaches in L.A, but when I was skating an exhibition in Sun Valley, she encountered Bob Paul. Bob met her two conditions: First, he was a good coach, and second, he would remember that the final call would always be my mom's. It takes a special kind of character to be a commanding teacher on the one hand and to know how to say "yes ma'am" on the other.

Bob had been an Olympic champion himself, he and his partner, Barbara Wagner, winning in the pairs for Canada at Squaw Valley in 1960. When we hooked up, he was trying to become an actor in L.A. To make ends meet Bob became a skating coach.

From the very start I liked him. I have worked with many coaches over the years, but whenever it has come time for me to work on a new signature piece, I always go to Bob. Even though I am not a big person (just about 5'4"), Bob made my skating and my skating presence look bigger than it was. Bob was also the first coach to teach me to combine the elements of skating into something more graceful. I was always inclined toward that on my own, and I have always looked to ballet stars for tips on how to hold my hands or my fingers in order to extend the line, which is so important to looking graceful and expressive. But Bob showed me how to cultivate that quality in myself.

Wispy costumes and flowing fabric would also help me enhance a longer line, but, basically, that long graceful style was inside me when I was doing toe turns in those basic little skating outfits. It was the way the music I liked to skate to made me move.

Bob understood all that, and he understood me. Together we would go to ballets and pick out moves that we wanted to work on. We saw the Bolshoi and the Kirov when they came to L.A. We both loved Margot Fonteyn, and we were influenced by her style. We listened to music and it was with Bob that I first fell in love with a piece I would keep coming back to in my skating: Tchaikovsky's symphony *"Pathétique."*

What Bob and I worked on was to take the *spirit* of ballet and incorporate it into skating. He was my coach, but he soon became my choreographer. Like my other coaches, he was dignified, handsome, and very put together, and he commanded respect. Just by being around him, I improved my posture, on and off the ice. Bob made me aware of my body position wherever I was. He was the one who suggested that I pull my hair back for a more classic look. Bob was the first of my coaches to help me create my own look.

Part of our success had to do with professional chemistry: When we were on a roll we could make up a routine in an hour. But personal chemistry played an equal role. In teenage-girl terms, I thought he was cute. When we first started working together, I suppose the attraction was all one way: me to him. As the years went by that attraction became more pronounced, although it never went anywhere but onto the ice.

Once though, when I was in my late teens, we were at my house listening to music and I remember him putting his arm around me. I definitely felt something and he did too, but my mom came home and that was the end of that. It might have gone further—if not that day, then another—but, in the end, keeping the attraction in the flirtation stage worked well for me in my skating. It brings a good energy to your work. When you are doing something soft and pretty and feminine, some romantic chemistry—a power boost of hormones—helps the piece.

This was an element that had to make its way slowly into my skating. If Mom and Dad didn't want anything racy in my costumes, the same went for my skating. While I was entering young womanhood, my mom kept her eagle eye out for anything that smacked of sensual exploration in my skating. Bob and I had to walk a fine line, but it was a side of me that come hell or high water was going to be expressed. And to be fair to Mom, she loved the balletic impulse in my work. She was just conflicted about my exploring the sensual side of art . . . and life.

But life wasn't all Olympics and suppressed puppy romance. There was still a little thing called high school, where my retiring personality hadn't changed all that much since grade school. Skating had given me a little more confidence, but I saved most of my expression for the ice. In school I was hardly noticed. Even going to my first Olympics hadn't changed things that much. Nobody seemed to treat me any differently.

My skating schedule got back to normal too. It took up every waking minute that I wasn't in school, easily five hours a day. I look back on it and wonder how on earth I ever worked that hard: I would get up at 4:45, throw my hair in a ponytail, and go to the rink until 8:00 A.M. There were plenty of days when I was tired, but I did it anyway. I figured I had done the big part by getting out of bed and getting dressed. Once that was done, I might as well get on with things. That way you don't have guilt the rest of the day. It's the same with my running or exercise routine today. Once you get into your jogging clothes and have your running shoes on . . . I just go on autopilot and get it done.

After school I went back to the rink, usually out to Burbank, where Bob Paul was teaching. I would put in another two or three hours before going home, having dinner, and doing my homework.

Where, you might ask, did I find time for an average teenage social life?

I didn't. Even though I was a budding romantic, I guess I was more in love with the idea of romance than with anybody in particular. A few of the boys who skated struck me as pretty cute, and sometimes a group of us would go swimming or to a movie, but it wasn't an official date. It was more a case of hanging out with friends.

In school, boys were completely off my radar screen.

Having a non-social life was just as well, I suppose, because, skating was my life. I wanted to be as good as my dedication and my teachers' lessons could make me.

Rarely, though, does anyone become truly great at anything without that one special teacher, the person who understands your abilities and your inner makeup so well that he or she can enable you to make the most use of the tools you were born with. I met that teacher, Carlo Fassi, in 1965.

He changed my skating, and he changed my life.

3

Carlo

*T*here has never been a greater pure skating coach than Carlo Fassi. After I trained with him, he went on to coach John Curry, Robin Cousins, and Dorothy Hamill. Carlo had style, skill, and personality. He was demonstrative in the way that Italians can be—very emotional when he spoke and always making big gestures. Recently I saw an old video of him following one of his students around on the ice, giving her pointers as she skated. He spoke a mile a minute and would get excited. As I think back on those times I hardly know how we understood Carlo in his broken English with a good dose of Italian thrown in.

The reason we understood him was he spoke skating, and so did we.

Carlo first saw me at the Junior Nationals in Long Beach, California, and he was impressed with my performance. "I have just seen a beautiful young skater from California," he told his wife, Christa. "Her name is Peggy Fleming."

Bob Paul had worked so well on bringing out my speed and posture—my dancer's back—but in 1965, Mom wanted a coach who could work on my weakness, school figures. Mom called Carlo, met with him, and it was decided: I would skate with Carlo, and the whole family would move to Colorado! Carlo's wife, Christa, thought this was absolutely extraordinary—to pick up the whole family and move so that a daughter could have the right skating coach—but from my family's point of view, having a family member as a National Champion in the Olympics was pretty big-time. The whole family was in favor of the move.

All in all, Colorado was a nice adventure for the Flemings My sister, Maxine, got into skiing, and both she and Janice baby-sat at the Broadmoor Hotel, where I was training. The Broadmoor paid baby-sitters well, all things considered, and I certainly wasn't bringing in any money: In those days Olympic athletes had to be one hundred percent amateur or they would be banned from competition.

The Broadmoor Hotel was pretty as a postcard, and the facilities were unbelievable. Thayer Tutt had created a 5-star, big and rambling, Rocky Mountain resort that was filled with his warm, larger-than-life personality. Because of the high altitude, training there built up your endurance, but the conditions were hardly what I would call rugged. The rink—it was called the World Arena—was an indoor rink that was in a separate building in the hotel complex. When we practiced we often had an audience from the convention and vacation crowd that came to stay at the hotel. Sometimes, for the bigger groups, we would put on an exhibition, which was great practice for staying loose in front of a crowd.

In my chartreuse dress
on the cover of *Life*
magazine. (© Art
Rickerby/*Life* magazine)

The morning after I
won the gold medal,
Sports Illustrated shot
this cover photo.
(© John G. Zimmerman/
Sports Illustrated)

My mom, Doris, at about 20 years old, while she was still a career girl working at the *San Francisco Chronicle*. (Collection of the author)

My dad, Al, in the Marine photo he gave to his mom. (Collection of the author)

Me and my sister Janice at the farm in Morgan Hill in 1952. (Collection of the author)

The four Fleming sisters in front of our family car. From left: Maxine, Peggy, Janice, and Cathy. (Collection of the author)

One of the earliest photos of me on skates, this picture was taken in 1959, on a rubber mat. (Courtesy of William Udell)

The geek years: a photo series taken in 1962. (Courtesy of William Udell)

My choreographer, Bob Turk, always good for a laugh, teaches me some moves in 1964. (Courtesy of William Udell)

A picture of me from *Life* magazine on January 24, 1964, right after I won my first U.S. National title in Cleveland, Ohio. (Photo by Art Shay/ *Life* Magazine)

My mom, in the second row, watches me intently from the stands at the 1965 World Championships. (Courtesy of William Udell)

Me in the official 1964 U.S. Olympic parade outfit. (Courtesy of William Udell)

With my coach, Bob Paul, in 1965 in Colorado Springs at my second Worlds competition, where I came in third. (Courtesy of William Udell)

Me in the "Ave Maria" skating costume sewn by my mom in 1966. (Courtesy of William Udell)

Doing school figures at the 1966 World Championships in Davos, Switzerland.
This picture was the model for a statue of skaters in San Jose, California.
(Collection of the author)

Carlo Fassi and I study my school figures on the Colorado College outdoor rink in 1968. (Collection of the author)

A signed picture of me for Greg, right before the 1968 Olympics.
(Collection of the author)

Carlo seen over my shoulder as I am getting my marks after my long program at the 1968 Worlds, my last amateur competition. (Courtesy of ABC Sports)

At the 1968 Olympics, having just finished my school figures, with Carlo on my right. (Collection of the author)

The 1968 World Championships in Geneva, Switzerland. From left: the Pairs champions, Ludmila Belousova and Oleg Protopopov; the Ladies champ, me; the Men's champ, Emmerich Danzer. (Courtesy of AP/Wide World Photos)

The happy couple: a photo of us at our wedding on June 13, 1970. (Collection of the author)

Gene Kelly serenading me in 1968 by singing "Peg O' My Heart" on my first television special. Notice our matching bow ties! (Courtesy of Bob Banner)

On a break with Andy Williams, who sang "Something in the Way She Moves" for my 1972 television special, "To Europe With Love." (Courtesy of Bob Banner)

Snoopy, Charles M. Schulz, and me in the role of Charlie Brown for a television special. (Photo by Christie Jenkins/Los Angeles)

I've been immortalized in the Peanuts comic strip! (Courtesy of Charles M. Schulz)

A Bob Mackie dress for Concert on Ice, 1972. (Courtesy of Bob Banner)

Paul Sibley lifts me as the swan during a 1972 Concert on Ice performance of *Swan Lake*. (Copyright Manfred D. Loose)

Performing at the L.A. Forum Ice Follies in 1976. This costume, designed by Pete Menefee, was supposed to hide my fifth-month pregnancy. I took a hiatus not too long afterward. (Photo by Fred L. Tate)

An "outer space" costume designed by Jef Billings for the 1981 Concert on Ice. (Courtesy of Bob Banner)

And then there was the ice: It was absolutely perfect, gray-ish in color, and you could see your figures as clearly as if you had painted them with a brush. Most of all—and this was a real-ly big blessing—Carlo decided that I was not the world's best morning person. I could go through the rote practice part of my training at six in the morning, but my brain wasn't fully awake yet, so Carlo would not start teaching me until eight or nine. "How are you going to learn if you are not awake?" he asked.

Carlo was, as I said, a sharp dresser. He also demanded that his pupils be well dressed. He let it be known that you weren't going to practice with him in a T-shirt and scraggly hair. "Dressing well on the ice puts you in a competition frame of mind," he explained. That way when you showed up at the Nationals or the Olympics with your hair done and a pretty costume, it didn't feel so foreign.

Carlo's neatness thing influenced every aspect of my skating. In addition to having perfect ice, and trying to look perfect in the way I dressed and carried myself, I wanted my skates to be per-fect whenever I went on the ice—whether it was practice or com-petition. Before every practice I would always check to make sure that my skates were perfectly polished and white as could be.

The attention to detail and neatness affected my school fig-ures too. Even if my form wasn't always perfect, my patch was neat and the figure I left on the ice was as neat as a human being could make it. In fact, sometimes Carlo would come over and touch up my patch, brushing away ice shavings so it looked even more perfect. That way if a competitor came over to check my patches, the neatness would psyche them out a little.

All my coaches contributed to my growth as a skater, but everything finally came together for me at the Broadmoor with Carlo. I got stronger in the altitude, my school figures improved, my new skating routine had a lot more substance, and I was skating better. Carlo was so secure as a coach that he had no problem with my continuing to work on my choreography with Bob Paul. Carlo knew that choreography and artistic interpretation weren't his strong points, so he let me work with Bob on that aspect of my skating. Before that I had never heard of a coach letting one of his skaters work with a different choreographer. They all wanted total control.

But Carlo didn't want that and didn't need it. He knew I wasn't going to leave him. I was making too much progress with him to dare dream of a move. Carlo's strengths were in technique and conditioning. His training made me strong and it made me consistent. Every day he had me go through my complete routine—from the start, Tchaikovsky's *"Pathétique,"* to the finale, Rossini's *La Gazza Ladra*. That was the routine I skated to championship after championship in my next four years, with Carlo as my coach and Bob as my choreographer.

By the time the summer of 1965 rolled around, I had been with Carlo only a short while, but I was invited on a European exhibition tour. Carlo had two young pupils from Texas, a girl and her brother, named Jenkins. That brother, Greg, was going to be in Europe with some college pals, and Carlo mentioned that he wouldn't mind if Greg checked up on me in Davos, Switzerland. So Greg sent me a letter in Colorado saying he would be in Davos too. For some reason, I kept that letter.

I certainly didn't have a clue that Greg Jenkins was going to become my boyfriend, much less my husband.

Greg came to my Davos exhibition and introduced himself afterward. He seemed like a nice guy, and the fact that he was another one of Carlo's students established a bond of sorts. When he offered to walk me home and carry my skates, I was very pleased. I had been invited to a banquet that the skating organization was throwing, and I suppose I might have invited Greg. Greg later told me that he went home to his college-guy-on-the-road hotel room and had cheese and crackers.

When we returned to the States, I wasn't really thinking about Greg, or any boy for that matter, but circumstances—or fate—seemed to want Greg and me to become interested in each other. His skating partner, Candy Coburn was from California, and we knew her from our years there. Mom offered to have her stay with us, which made Candy's mother feel really comfortable; but she was still too young to have a driver's license, so Greg would stop by and pick her up on the way to practice. I got used to seeing Greg sitting around the house, waiting for his partner to get ready. He still does the same thing today—sits around and waits for me to get ready. Sometime that fall, Sandi Sells, a skater and close friend of the Jenkins family in Dallas, also came to stay in the Doris Fleming semiofficial sorority house for young skaters.

Sandi was the first to think that Greg and I would make a good couple, and she would often say nice things to me about Greg. After a while, I started to pay attention to him. One day at the end of December—the twenty-ninth, to be exact—Greg asked me out on a date. We went to a movie, *The Sound of Music,* and he tried to hold my hand.

He was successful.

Two days later he asked me out for New Year's Eve. We went to a party with some friends, and at midnight we all watched the fireworks show on Pike's Peak. Greg turned to me, and before I knew it, he had kissed me. I wasn't a very experienced kisser at that point so it was just a quickie, but it was a real honest-to-god kiss.

That was the beginning of the longest relationship in my life. Thirty-four years later, it is still growing. But back then, on the way to my second Olympics, my love life was going to have to take a back seat to skating. Even if I wasn't sure about that, Doris Fleming was—and she was still definitely the boss. The next goal for me was to win the World Championship.

When you are the reigning World Champion, it's almost as if the prize is yours to lose. In 1965 Petra Burke, a muscular Canadian with a repertoire of enormous jumps, was the reigning champion, a big skater with big moves. I wasn't big, but all my training was toward skating big and light, and I thought the world was ready for that.

But between 1965 and 1966 something happened to Petra. Unhappy with her figure, she went on a crash diet and showed up as a less powerful-looking skater. As the time approached for the World Championship in Davos, it was clear that Petra's crown was there for the taking. She had lost weight, and she had also lost her command over the ice. This was my chance to win the title. My mother knew it and Carlo knew it too. Being a European, he looked at the competition as a home game. He knew what it would take to position me as the favorite, and what it would take to have the judges see my skating the way Carlo and I wanted them to.

The Davos competition would be held outside in the winter, in the Alps, so it was going to be cold. Good-bye nice warm training rink. Carlo wanted me to toughen up and get used to skating outside in freezing weather, which was consistent with his philosophy of making practice as close as possible to actual competition conditions.

On many cold Rocky Mountain nights, we trooped over to the outdoor hockey rink. Carlo flipped on the lights and I would take to the ice in a light outfit. Let me tell you, skating at night in the Colorado Rockies when it is twenty degrees outside is pretty chilly. But Greg—who was studying at Colorado College—came down to watch me in the stands.

Somehow having as my audience a handsome guy whom I was getting to like made it seem not so cold. I had an extra incentive to stand straighter, to wear something prettier. When Greg showed up with some of his college buddies, I responded even more to my private audience.

Of course there was more to my training than a survival course in outdoor night skating. My program was the point of it all: Bob's choreography, Carlo's obsession with execution, and my growing sense of what my skating could be. I was evolving a style of skating "big but light," and I was also developing a pace and rhythm to those four minutes on the ice that were my free skate, my Long Program.

I approached it as I do most tasks in life: You can't skate full out for four minutes anymore than you can do anything else at maximum output. Timing and pacing is nearly as important as the actual moves you attempt. I tend to spread my energy through the routine, trying to get most of the really hard stuff out of the way at the top of the performance while my energy level is still at it's highest. It grabs the attention of the crowd. You really want to try to get a "Wow!" out of the audience. I have no question in my mind that the judges respond to an audience that is genuinely thrilled by a well-executed, difficult move. After that I go into some of the more flowing, less physically demanding stuff. When I say less physically demanding, it's all relative—none of this stuff can be done if you are in less than top condition. But the more flowing segment is a chance to restore your strength after coming out of the box with your really big moves. Finally it is very important that you complete the range of emotions by giving the audience, and the judges, something big and exciting at the end.

Carlo was a practice-makes-perfect kind of coach, but he had an artist's sense of the right mix, like a symphony conductor trying to combine an orchestra of wind, ice, sun, music, an audience, judges and, of course, a skater into four minutes of magic.

When we got to Davos, he became even more of a stickler: The sunshine was so bright and the mountains so white that the combination of bright light on white ice was nearly blinding, My blue eyes are very sensitive to light; I almost always sneeze when I go into bright daylight. I had a tough time getting used to seeing where I was going at Davos. Carlo wanted me on the ice as much as possible so that I would get accustomed to the glare. But not if there was a strong wind—Carlo didn't want me throwing my timing off. It may sound unthinkable for a coach to tell an athlete not to practice right before the biggest event of her life, but Carlo did just that. "Relax," he would say, "visualize what you are going to do. It will help you more than going out on the ice under the wrong conditions."

I did all of that, but I was nervous. I knew the championship was there for me to take, and the pressure and anxiety were getting to me. My mother had some clever ruses for dealing with me when the pressure started to take its toll. Instead of comforting me and saying, "Hey, Peggy, it will all be fine," she would pick a fight. I would flare up in anger, then I would break down and cry, and then, *poof,* like a release valve that started to quiet my tension and fear, I was ready to compete . . . still somewhat nervous, but otherwise ready.

Mom and I had had a real humdinger of a fight in Davos. I was sitting in my room one day reading some of the letters that

Greg had sent me. By this time Greg and I were definitely an item. I had all his letters out and I was spending a very long time trying to write a great letter back.

Mom came in the room and blew her stack. "You're not here to swoon over your boyfriend. You are here to win a World Championship." With that, she took all of Greg's pictures and ripped them up.

Mom and I went at each other with heated words. She had gotten to me, and when someone gets to me, I become determined: I was going to show her she was wrong, that I wasn't frivolous.

I was so mad I could hardly speak. I cried and cried. I Scotch-taped Greg's pictures back together, getting tears all over them as I did.

I thought my mom was being selfish and cruel, but she was right. I *wasn't* focused and getting me mad was just the right medicine. Mom, above all others, knew what made me tick. When I get mad, I get tougher and work harder—if only to show "them" that they are wrong and I am right. My mother used my anger as a tool. If I was lazy, or had a bad case of nerves before I performed, Mom would always pick a fight. I would cry, the tension would go away, and I would skate my best.

I hated it when she did that, but kids never believe their parents are smarter than them about some things. I went for a walk, collected myself, and made myself focus on the program. I fought back the fear that I always faced whenever they called my name right before I began my program.

Somehow, the combination of Carlo's coaching and my Mom's heavy emotional artillery worked magic and drew a great performance out of me—I went out and won my first World Championship so I guess I have to admit my mom was right—darn it!

After Davos, I got my first taste of the overscheduling that has since become my normal life. Before we left for Europe, I had committed to an exhibition for the Boston Skating Club, a renowned and wonderful organization. It seemed like an easy commitment. My original plan was to go to Davos and stop in for the Boston event on my way home to Colorado.

The one thing I hadn't counted on was winning—because with that came a commitment to tour through Europe and the Soviet Union.

I could easily have begged off, and everyone in Boston would have understood, but I have always believed that when you commit to something, you do it. I read somewhere that Woody Allen once said that eighty percent of success in show business is simply showing up. I couldn't agree more, and it doesn't stop with show business. If you say you are going to be there, you do whatever you have to do and you show up.

As it turned out, I would not have forgiven myself if I hadn't. Dad, who never could get the time off (or the money) to fly to Europe, was going to make a special trip to Boston to see me.

Just for him, I planned on skating "Ave Maria," which was his favorite. It was, and remains, one of mine as well. I had seen a German couple perform to it on one of my first exhibition tours in Europe. I could really feel the music and I wanted to try to create a piece of my own. Bob Turk and I set to work, and it became my first piece that was truly balletic in its inspiration. The music was haunting and the skating was linked to the music. It wasn't just a general background melody. Giving life to music through skating was something I wanted to be known for.

I had already skated "Ave Maria" at a number of exhibitions before the time Dad showed up in Boston. He was so proud of my having won the Worlds. Even though he wasn't a steady churchgoer, he had still grown up Catholic. Seeing his daughter in white skating to deeply devotional music and knowing that I was the World Champion filled him with pride.

That was the last time my father saw me skate. A few weeks later when I was traveling and skating in Europe, Mom and I received word that his bad health habits had finally caught up with him. Dad died from his third heart attack.

You see what I mean about the importance of showing up? To this day, I am thankful that I got to give my father that last performance.

In those years, my skating was what these days we call "in the zone." I was skating better and better. My style was very much my own and very much in tune with the times. Audiences liked it. Judges liked it. I continued to win a string of National and World Championships that eventually took me to the Olympics.

But I never coasted. Carlo would not stand for it,. Mom wouldn't stand for it, and neither would I. Carlo really bore down on me, and I responded by taking my performance to a higher level. Carlo raised the bar by getting me to do the same thing over and over again until I was consistent. Just as I had done when I was younger with Gene Turner and Bob Turk, I tried to make a game out of the lessons: Winning meant executing a perfect move, having a perfect lesson. If Carlo asked for a double axel in practice, I did my best to give him one. If he asked for another, I never questioned why, I just tried to land another perfect one. By trying for perfection in my training I was seeking to erase the line between practice and performance. This was my way of internalizing Carlo's principle of making every session as close to real competition as possible.

I was growing as a skater, but I was also growing as a woman and that affected my skating. As Greg and I became more serious, I gained a new kind of confidence—confidence as a woman that translated into more expression in my skating. I was feeling the music more. When your heart starts to stir, you are more open to music, which speaks straight to the heart. Skating is first and foremost a sport, but there is a tremendous artistic and emotional component to it. Having new and deeper feelings made me want to put them into my skating, although sometimes my feelings ran a couple beats ahead of my artistic and technical abilities.

Since I was feeling romantic, I decided to skate in a new costume, and Bob choreographed a new number for me. It was Adam's *Giselle*, which was one of the compositions that he and I had both loved when we first started to work together. *Giselle* was a much more balletic piece than anything I had tried before. I loved it, but the audiences and the skating world sensed that in some way I was over my head. Bob and I hadn't given it enough time to work everything out, and I had a new costume to boot. It was a big change in style for the audience to accept. Even though I won my next National Championship with *Giselle* in the program, I listened to my critics and decided not to use it for the Worlds in Vienna. I went back to the program that I had been skating since 1965.

Vienna looked to me like the classic picture you have in your mind of Europe, especially in winter: the old buildings, the cafés, all very romantic and old world. Our hotel overlooked the two rinks, a practice rink and a performance rink. For most of our stay, rain and unpredictable weather made for terrible ice conditions. On the evening of my event, it was very cold and the warm-up ice was very crunchy and kind of slow. For some reason we were not allowed on the performance ice until we competed.

You may have noticed when you watch a televised event that all the skaters are given time to warm up on the performance ice before they compete. But in Vienna, the ice on the practice rink was dimly lit and the performance ice was bright and glaring, so it was very disorienting. I didn't have much chance to gauge how the ice affected the other skaters because I drew second.

Oh well, I thought, nothing to be done except to get out there and do it. I promptly skated right into the bang boards on one of my first moves and fell to the ice on the first double axel. I'm sure there are worse feelings in the world, but to be the top skater in the world, competing to retain your title, and to stumble and butt slide is not a fun thing.

I picked myself up and went on. It crossed my mind that I had blown the event, but I refused to let that shake me. I remember saying to myself, "You know this stuff. You have skated it perfectly before. Just do it again."

I did. I won my second World championship.

The next step was the Nationals in Philadelphia, which enabled me to go to the Olympics on a high note. I could not have done better. The routine that I had worked on all these years and the new style I had been creating with Carlo and Bob finally came to full flower.

If there was ever a championship that I was meant to win, it was that National title in Philadelphia in 1968. I couldn't wait to show everyone how much I had worked that past year. For the first time, I wasn't that nervous. My training had gone well, and I had avoided injuries, which are the great fear in competition. Everything felt right. I just knew when I stepped onto the ice that I was going to be great. I couldn't wait for the music to start, and when it did, I had a feeling of ease, comfort, and flow. The jumps seemed effortless, and the crowd gave me adrenaline that felt like it was physically lifting each jump higher. From beginning to end I remember one thing, one constant in my performance: *I am completely enjoying this.*

I have seen two performances in my life I will never forget, performances that people concede were among the greatest skating they have ever witnessed. One was Brian Boitano's breathtaking gold medal program in Calgary. He was so majestic and in command that you knew from the start it would be flawless. The other was Michelle Kwan's at the Nationals in 1998—again, a blend of power and grace that left me in a state of wonderment. People who were in Philadelphia in 1968 have said the same thing about my performance being one of the great ones. I was too busy skating, of course, to be able to experience it as I did Michelle's and Brian's great efforts.

After my victory, I skated "Ave Maria" in the postcompetition exhibition. The music moved me as never before. The song is a glimpse of heaven, and I was there from the first note until the last—especially the last. I remember extending my arm on the last note, a long, languid lift of the arm and a wave of the wrist. I made it last as long as possible—long after the last note had died. For a long instant, the crowd was as quiet as a congregation in prayer. And then, when I broke the spell, the applause filled me with joy. If you ever get a moment that joyous in life, you must treasure it.

I was off to the Olympics with all the confidence in the world and, with Mom's help, a new dress too.

As I mentioned earlier, my parents were always dead set against makeup, stockings, and anything that would be considered remotely provocative. The word *sexy* was almost too sexy to be spoken in our house, which was hard on me as a competitor. After all, if I was trying to project something feminine and beautiful in my skating, it seemed kind of important to be able to project that femininity to the last row in the audience. Even the best-looking woman in the world can use a little help from the wardrobe and makeup departments.

I wanted to feel pretty in Grenoble . . . and sexy. I wanted to wear something tight, so it would show off the lines of my body—the lines that I was trying to extend into my performance. If I had asked Mom to make me something that showed a lot of my body, she wouldn't have done it in a million years, but "tight" didn't bother her because I was still covered up, so we went for tight.

Mom worried about that chartreuse dress until the last second, sewing until I had to dress for the competition, but Carlo and I were much more concerned with getting my skating to where it needed to be to win the gold that the world expected me to win.

At my first Olympics, in 1964, I had simply been glad to be there. But things were different in 1968. I was now the queen of the ice. Anything less than a gold medal would have been viewed as failure. On top of that, America didn't have too many odds-on favorites that year. If a member of the United States Team were going to win a gold medal, it looked as if I were going to have to be the one to do it.

Nineteen sixty-eight was the most intense year of the Vietnam War, the year of the deaths of Martin Luther King and Bobby Kennedy. America was looking for a good-news story. Everyone wanted a little relief from the grim headlines. As a regular American girl from a modest background, I was supposed to be the designated feel-good headline.

Mom and I decided that I could stay at the village with the other athletes, but that I would move in with her a few days before the competition. Sure, the athlete's village had been fun in 1964, but this time neither she nor I was concerned about having fun. Getting a good night's sleep was more important and that wasn't going to happen in the village, where the beds were barely a step above an army cot. Also, the Olympic village is probably the world's best spreader of the flu. I had a touch of it in 1964, and even though I was happy with sixth place, I know I could have skated better had I been healthier. I didn't want any distractions or any diseases in Grenoble.

I came out of semiseclusion for the competition. My school figures had never been better, and I aced the compulsories. But to win I needed a good free skate—the Long Program I had honed for the last four years. I skated well enough to win but not nearly as well as I had in Philadelphia. Somehow, less than perfect that day brought me something that perfect in Philadelphia couldn't give me: an Olympic gold.

Shortly after they announced the scores, they presented the medals. That honor fell to Avery Brundage, the crusty old chairman of the International Olympic Committee, the great champion of amateurism. As long as he had anything to do with it there would be no "dream teams" in basketball or anything else that even vaguely smacked of professionalism. It would defile the purity of the Olympic spirit.

When Mr. Brundage gave us our medals, he leaned over and gave each girl a kiss, as was his custom. At the news conference afterward I was asked how he kissed.

I gave it a beat and thought "what a weird question!' Then answered in my best deadpan: "He was an amateur."

I would not be an amateur very much longer.

4

My Long Program Really Begins

*T*he years of lessons, the competitions, the Olympics—in a sense those were the compulsories in my life. Now that I had won my gold, doors opened up that required choices. In the beginning, I had help making them, especially from Mom, but ultimately it was my life and my choices.

As the last notes of Rossini's *La Gazza Ladra* died away on the Olympic ice, my life as an amateur was coming to a close. I still had one more amateur competition to go—the World Championship, which I won two weeks later—but the Olympic gold was the event that changed my life. I would no longer have to follow the routine I had followed since I was a little girl: skate/school/skate, with Mom and my coaches telling me when to start, when to stop, and what to do next.

Now, at the age of nineteen I was done with childhood. I had not suddenly become mature or emotionally independent, but instant fame and the faint beginnings of fortune demanded that I begin the Long Program known as the rest of my life.

The morning after my victory—when I was still riding the emotional high of winning—I went to have my picture taken for the cover of *Sports Illustrated*. As I look at it now, I see an innocent and enthusiastic teenager trying to look as feminine and graceful as I could in my tight green dress. People responded to that picture with equal enthusiasm.

Winning the gold at the Olympics on international television followed by *Life* magazine and *Sports Illustrated* covers brought attention to me that previous skaters had never enjoyed. But a single phone call made to my mom within hours of my winning the gold medal was the one element that opened up the door to an opportunity that other skaters never had: a television career.

The call came from Bob Banner—another in the line of well spoken and distinguished-looking men who have stepped into my life to influence me. Bob is a Hollywood producer, but he's never been one of those fast-talking love-ya-baby show business guys. If he had been, Doris Fleming would have gotten rid of him in a hurry.

I don't even think I had time to shower after my free skate when he called Mom in Grenoble with an offer from NBC for a special starring . . . me! Nobody had ever done this before. Perry Como or Andy Williams did NBC specials, not ice skaters. That's what I mean about being lucky.

NBC's offer hadn't quite come as a bolt out of the blue, though. Bob Banner—who had made a very big name as the producer of *The Carol Burnett Show*—had been following me for some time. He was a frequent guest at the Broadmoor Hotel in the years that I trained there, and he first saw me after Carol Burnett had played the performing arts center that was across from our rink. That was what was one of the things I loved about the rink—there was always an interesting crowd of people coming in. They may have been there for a convention, or on vacation, or as part of the cast of whatever was playing at the performing arts center. Many of them liked to sit in the stands and watch serious skaters training. The skaters and Carlo liked it because we always had the pressure of an audience watching us during our training. Carlo liked anything that made it feel more like competition.

Bob was very taken with my skating. He once told an interviewer about the first time he saw me: "I went to watch the ice show and out skated a young lady who didn't look like a skater and didn't act like a skater. She acted like a ballerina, so beautiful and so lovely. I asked a couple of the people there, 'Who is this person?' They said, 'Well, her name is Peggy Fleming.'"

Bob went over to my mom and introduced himself. My mother liked his low-key Texas manner and the way he asked about me. This was two years before the Olympics. I suppose he had the germ of a TV idea for me in his head, but he also was genuinely interested in me. My mother had great antenna for people who wanted to get to me. Bob passed her test. She trusted him, although if you tell Bob that he will let you know that he thought my mom was one of the most protective and untrusting people he ever ran into. Letting go when it came to me and my career was impossible for her. She had the same problem when I began to mature and began to take more control of my career. She was in the habit of thinking for me and protecting me from every danger—real or imagined. But that was Doris Fleming for you—fiercely protective and always on her guard in a world that she felt was full of sharks (for the most part she was probably right).

Thank goodness she liked Bob! After we won the Olympics— that victory was definitely a "we"; me, Carlo, and Mom—we had all kinds of offers, and Bob was a good standard against which to measure the rest of the producers, promoters, and programmers that materialized. It was a lucky day when I met Bob and another lucky day when he came to me with the TV offers.

As I said, I was the first skater to have that kind of opportunity. Before then, all you could do was the ice shows. True, Sonja Henie had gone to Hollywood and made movies—and so had Esther Williams—but they were the only women who had made the transition from the Olympics to stardom in the entertainment world. Carol Heiss had tried to do the same. Although she had talent, beauty, and a great personality, the only film she ever got to do was *Snow White and the Three Stooges*. On the guy side, Johnny Weismuller had gone from swimming to being Tarzan, but for the most part, athletics had never been any kind of stepping-stone to success in the world of entertainment. All things considered, it seemed to Mom and me that TV was there for the asking while movies were the longest of long shots.

There was another benefit to television. It meant I didn't have to go right into the ice shows. Although I did ultimately skate in a number of them, including my own, at that point in time it would have meant signing on for a full-time commitment that would have left me little room to pursue anything else. So at the first stages of planning a career—even taking the initial steps—we wanted to do something that would open the doors that TV offered rather than closing them.

Having my own television special meant I could do something more than the ice shows and a coaching career.

My choices would have been extremely limited had I tried to go into the movies. What could I have done in 1968? Be a James Bond girl who gets bumped off in the last ten minutes (which means no sequel)? Be Elvis's girlfriend and stand around and smile and make big eyes while he sings?

On "Here's Peggy Fleming," my first TV special, Gene Kelly was my guest star. Gene Kelly! Like everyone else, I had always loved his work: He combined grace and athleticism in dance in the same way that I aspired to combine them in skating. Like me, he wasn't tall, but his style gave his moves a long line. He had an easygoing Irish way about him that reminded me of my dad, who would have just loved to hear Gene Kelly sing "Peg O' My Heart."

And then there were the clothes I got to wear on television. Going from the Simplicity and McCall's catalogue as interpreted by Mom to having Bob Mackie design dresses just for me was about as glamorous as it gets. Bob had never done any skating outfits before so it was a big change for him too. And it was a *huge* change for my mom to have someone else making my costumes. It was the first time she had to relinquish control of an aspect of my career, and she didn't do that easily. She came to every fitting and offered her thoughts at every step of the way. Although the costumes were stunning, I think Bob probably held back a little because Mom wasn't about to let me wear anything that she thought was provocative. It never crossed her mind that *anything* you put on a nineteen-year-old girl has a good chance of being provocative.

It was a new world for me, but in many ways it was not that different from the one I had grown up in. Instead of a coach and a choreographer, I had a producer and a director, still telling me, "Try that one more time, Peggy!" As always, someone gave the orders and I skated.

' But the single event that demonstrated my new position in the world was when Katharine Hepburn showed up at our set on the MGM lot. Like millions of women, I held Katharine Hepburn up as the ideal of style: so casual, so womanly, yet so at ease and unglitzy.

"I wanted to meet you," she said as she introduced herself.

I was astonished. I finally realized that the Olympic medal had put me in a realm that was very special. I never thought that Katherine Hepburn would be eager to meet anyone, much less me. Even though I still felt very much like the shy little girl I had been in Morgan Hill, it was becoming apparent that the world saw me as a glamorous young woman. I had to figure out how to live up to that image in my television shows, while in my real life I had to try just as hard to lead a normal existence. We moved into a new home in Los Angeles, which I was able to buy for the family with my first television and endorsement checks, and I began to get more serious about my relationship with Greg.

That first NBC special did well in the ratings so the network ordered more, and I ended up doing one each year for the next four years. Those shows were filmed on location. Being outside on location added a visual element to the shows: the beauty of the outdoors in places like Sun Valley, Idaho, and the glamour of fairytale locations like St. Petersburg, Russia. The fact that we shot on film was another lucky break for me. I have always been concerned with the look of my skating, and skating on film is much more beautiful than videotape, which has a harsher quality to it. The cameramen and lighting people were much better at getting a beautiful look on film than even the best tape has still to this day. The shows looked gorgeous and showed me off to my best.

Anything that looks graceful and effortless and easy usually has a lot of grueling work behind it, and these shows were no exceptions. One of my favorite shows was the one we did in Sun Valley, the same town where Sonja Henie had starred in the movie *Sun Valley Serenade*. I have always liked contemporary music in addition to the classics, and for that show we had the Carpenters interpreting a number of Beatles songs. Not many people can get away with interpreting the Beatles, but Karen Carpenter was a tremendous creative spirit. I wished I could have spent more time getting to know her and her brother then, but when you are in the middle of a production, all you do is work. The Carpenters were in the studio. I was on the ice. We said hello a few times, but that was the extent of it. She did a version of "Help" in the middle of the show that was totally different than the Beatles' version, and the vulnerability in her voice still haunts me. Now that Karen is gone, it makes me remember that you have to appreciate people and opportunities when you have the chance. I never really got to tell her what a special show that was because of her, so I'm telling her now.

The show was also special because of the great French skier Jean-Claude Killy, who was my male counterpart as the gold medal pinup athlete from the Olympics. Bob Banner sat us in front of a roaring fireplace, where we improvised our scenes. If you were under the impression that we were two young people in the first stages of a love affair, that was the idea that Bob had in mind.

The highlight of that show was a lighthearted duet with an

"Anything You Can Do, I Can Do Better" feel which Jean-Claude and I performed on the rink and slopes of Sun Valley. We both skated, we both skied, and it is obvious in both cases who was the Olympic Champion.

When you see the show, it looks seamless: a great location, music by Irving Berlin, and beautiful ice. Getting it to look that way was a huge effort. The original idea was to shoot the scene during the day on a picturesque pond right in front of the lodge, beautifully set against the backdrop of the mountains behind the lodge. It was supposed to be beautiful. The only problem was that the warm Chinook winds blowing out of the west melted the ice during the day. The only way that we could film the sequence was to truck in tons and tons of crushed ice during the night: ice cubes, blocks of ice, shaved ice. I don't know if anyone in town could get a frozen margarita that week because we used all the ice cubes in town.

Our make-do ice was most skatable midnight until six A.M., so that was when we shot. "Skatable" is a relative term though—there is no way that five million ice cubes makes an ideal skating surface. In addition, the temperature was about minus sixteen degrees, so I was absolutely frozen to the marrow. Even worse, while we skated we could look into the lodge, its windows all aglow, fireplaces roaring, and folks having a nightcap. I was miserable, but when you see the finished product it is gorgeous, right down to the full moon shining overhead. They couldn't have made a more picture-pretty set on a Hollywood sound stage.

I vowed I would never skate under such freezing conditions again.

But what did I know? In television production there seems

to be a law of nature that says if there is a choice between easy conditions and tough conditions, you can bet on the tough ones. Sun Valley was like spring break in Fort Lauderdale compared to the show that we shot in Russia.

Bob was keen to do a show in Russia because so many wonderful skaters came from there. Mom loved the idea too, especially when she learned that this would be the first Soviet-American network TV show ever—a pretty big deal in those coldest days of the Cold War. I was excited too, to be in a country with a great skating tradition and, even more exciting for me, the greatest ballet tradition in the world.

When we arrived in Leningrad (not at that time St. Petersburg), I was treated like a movie star. The combination of being from big-time American TV and being the reigning woman skater in a country full of skaters made for a big welcome. People came to see me practice and asked for my autograph.

Warm as my reception was, Leningrad itself was cold. With wind chill at forty degrees below zero, I longed for the balmy days in Sun Valley, when it was a bearable sixteen below. Our scene was a half-mile out on the white ice of Finland Bay, which was nearly forty feet thick! They regularly drove buses and trucks out there, which chewed up the ice. We brought our own Zamboni, just like the one my dad used to drive to smooth the ice during my early morning practice sessions back in Pasadena.

I walked through the scene with Bob: I was wearing a fur hat, a big fluffy ski jacket, and fur-lined boots. I could not have been dressed any more warmly—and I was still freezing.

I took a deep breath, and the first words out of my mouth were, "I really don't know if I can do this. It's way too cold."

I went back to my dressing room and cried. I felt rotten about letting everyone down, but the cold felt like it could kill you. Then Bob came in and said, "Peggy, you don't really have to do this. If you don't think you can, it's okay."

That made up my mind. I was going to do it. We would shoot the scene in short spurts until I was cold, then I could go back to the Russian bus, where I would warm up again and we would shoot another little piece of my routine.

I waited in the bus until they called for me. I took a deep breath and screamed as the cold air hit my skin. I was good for three minutes, maximum, then I had to go back to the bus. The other skaters, who were all from the Russian Ice Ballet, said they couldn't believe I was skating outside in such cold weather—and these were Russians!

I am not exaggerating about how cold it was. My face turned red from the cold, and my nose and jaw actually turned purple. You wouldn't know that to look at the scene in the show, but I learned that makeup can do wonders for a woman. It took a lot of makeup to make me look normal.

When I got back to the hotel after the day's shooting, the only way I was able to warm up was to get into a hot tub, sip a little vodka, and chalk it up to character building. I had the feeling my dad would have approved.

I received a lot of press in Russia and star treatment, but that was not so surprising in a country where ice-skating is a major national pastime. The same isn't true of China, but when I went there a few years later with a group of nine American skaters, it was like I was Elvis. Everywhere I went I was mobbed. People were so starved for things from the West, and especially America. If a basketball team had come in our place, they would have received the same treatment.

We taped two exhibitions there. The audiences were tremendously enthusiastic. There was a stately sky box/VIP suite for the Red Chinese leader, Deng Xiao Ping, who sent word through the American Ambassador that he wanted to meet me. Chris Schenkel, the great ABC broadcaster, and I were ushered into the presence of Deng, who had to be helped to his chair. (I was told he had been offering toasts all afternoon) Poor Chris Schenkel! When Deng Xiao Ping offered him a toast, he couldn't refuse—you didn't do that in China. I remember Chris's eyes popping and his face turning red. Thankfully, I was skating, or I might have had to down a few shots along with Deng.

Deng was very courteous and, apparently, a big fan of mine. "We have many skating fans in China," he said through an interpreter. "We don't have so many televisions, so in the communes there will be hundreds of people watching one set. "

"How many people will be watching all over China?" I asked.

"Oh, about eight hundred million," he answered. To give you an idea of how big that audience is, it's about ten times the number that watches a Superbowl. But numbers like that are so incomprehensible that they are almost meaningless to me. Much more meaningful was one little girl who saw me on that trip, although it would be years before I knew about her.

Lu Chen, who would go on to be the world champion in 1995, is a breathtaking skater. She is beautiful, ethereal, and graceful. Her skating has everything that I have tried to include in my own, and I admire her about as much as I admire any skater I have ever seen. Apparently she saw videos of me skating during that trip to China and decided that she would try to emulate me. You can't have a more gratifying feeling as a performer and an athlete than to inspire a young athlete to greatness.

I enjoyed making ice skating shows for television, whether it was a big international event like the China tour or one of my specials. I couldn't have done that if I had, as skaters had done before me, gone straight from the Olympics to an exclusive contract with one of the ice shows. When I decided to begin appearing in the ice show, a few months after we wrapped the first NBC special, it was on my own terms, which was a big achievement for a skater. Previous Olympic medalists had no choice but to skate when the shows wanted them—a grueling nine- or ten-month schedule. I didn't want that life, although I did want to appear in public.

Mom worked very hard on making the right deal for me and when we finally signed the Ice Follies show, it required less than a full-time commitment. I was allowed to come and go, so that I would have time for television and endorsement work. Each time I appeared, a special insert was placed in the program.

Between the Olympic publicity and the awareness generated by my television show, I was able to ask for—and get—unprecedented money for a skater in an ice show. With the aid of our lawyer, Mom had wisely wangled a percentage of ticket sales as part of my deal. This was good for the show and good for me. It encouraged me to work very hard promoting the shows: I appeared on local television and radio and in magazine pieces, and it had the desired effect on my paycheck. It wasn't Michael Jordan money, or even anything close to what star skaters are paid now, but by the standards of those days it was astronomical—unheard of for a skater. I felt it was an important advance for all skaters, and for me it was a very nice paycheck.

When you come from no money—and my family had *no* money—it's really nice to have some, not only because you can afford nice things, although that's great, but also because it takes away that constant tension that had worn my father down. Being able to buy a new car *and* a new house was more than my dad could have dreamed of doing. I understood that skating was starting to be very good to me.

I'll take that a step further; Life was starting to be very good to me. Greg and I had gone from two kids who liked each other's company to two people who wanted to build a life together. With my home in California, my work taking me on the road so much, and Greg finishing medical school in Dallas, it wasn't the easiest romance to keep together, but I knew and he knew that this was the real thing.

I suppose Mom did too, which was why she didn't stand in the way. I know she perceived Greg as a threat to her. He was going to take me away from her. In Mom's view, any distancing of me from her would also represent a danger for my career. But how much better could it get than a young doctor who had been a serious skater himself, who had the good sense to stay out of my mother's way? Mom was the boss of my career and, for the time being, Greg had no problem with that. He knew that was what it took to smooth the way to marriage.

I was the one getting married, but Mom was the one making the wedding. I was so busy with my career, and Greg was so deep into his spring semester of med school that we were glad, in a way, to have Mom take care of things. It made her feel she was in control, and it gave her something to do.

As with most things, she took the reins and produced the whole thing down to the last detail. I just let her do it. It was the price of peace, and for me, the big picture was the important thing—the marriage, not the wedding. Looking back, though, if I had had the self-assurance then that I have now, I wouldn't have let Mom totally run the show. I would never have put up with her not letting Greg's brother, Philip, in the wedding party just because he had a beard. For some reason that I never could figure out, she also forbade Greg's sister, Christie, from being in the wedding party too. Instead of fighting, we let her have her way.

I wish, now, that we had stood our ground because those kinds of slights take years to overcome.

Mom wanted to make me the kind of fantasy wedding she dreamed of when she was a little girl. Through some friends, she arranged it at the Bel Air Country Club, one of the prettiest and most upper-crust places in Los Angeles. Of course, Mom, who had made all my skating costumes for years, wanted to pick out my dress. I wouldn't have been surprised if she asked to come along on the honeymoon, but it never got to that point. I stood my ground on the dress: I told Mom I wanted to pick out my own dress, and I told Bob Mackie the same thing when he very graciously offered to make a dress for me.

What I wanted was a wedding dress that looked like a wedding dress, the dress every girl imagines. Mom, Maxine—who was my maid of honor—and I went to a bridal shop. I picked out a very typical wedding dress with a long train and a veil, and with short sleeves that I thought made it kind of sporty. It was more cute than fairy princess.

The wedding itself was beautiful, and the honeymoon was the first time that Greg and I had spent twenty-four hours together. It was also my first real vacation where I actually got to check into a nice hotel with no other purpose than to have a good time. Kona Village in Hawaii has become just about our favorite place in the world. It's so restful and simple: a bunch of private huts with no keys, no locks, no TV, no radio, but it has a beautiful sandy beach with comfy hammocks. To those of you who don't believe you can have second, third, fourth, and fifth honeymoons, I am happy to report that we have done that—and then some—on return visits to Kona village. We spent two weeks there on our first visit, and then it was back to work at Ice Follies as well as continuing my string of TV specials.

From Ice Follies I went to Holiday on Ice—different name, but basically the same kind of show. There was an attitude among a lot of the amateur skaters who had been in competition that ice shows weren't real skating. The stuff we did in the competitions as amateurs was what they thought of as real skating. I had a little of that attitude in me too, but I got over it. I mean, was competition somehow better just because we didn't get paid? Working for free is not necessarily more artistic than getting paid for working.

I challenged myself in the ice shows, just as Carlo had demanded, and just as I demanded of myself years before Carlo, that every practice should be a perfect practice. I was still a little nervous before I went on the ice, but it was nothing like competition nerves. In competition it's almost as if they go out of their way to make you feel ill at ease. In the ice shows we were like a family putting on a show. You got used to the same people backstage. You knew the lighting people would hit their cues when they were supposed to. You got used to the pace of the show and when Susie Berens started the cowboy production number I knew I had to start getting into my costume and skates.

Once I had figured out that the only way I could do the ice

shows was to take the performing part seriously, the most difficult part of those years was learning how to pace myself for a seven-day-a-week schedule. People who are not on the road so much think that it is wonderful and glamorous to travel around the world to famous places. They think that you get to go to all the museums and you shop at famous boutiques. But frankly, when you are going from airport to airport, hotel room to hotel room, and arena to arena, you have neither the time nor the energy. I learned how to save my energy during the day. I learned when, what, and what not to eat so that I was at my peak when I was on the ice. Getting to my peak became a game for me and I always to try to win every game I play.

The best, and most difficult, day of the week was always Saturday.

I used to hate Saturday mornings because we would have to be there early for the ten A.M. show. I would have to pace myself because I still had two more shows to do that day. By the two o'clock, I was warmed up already, but I still had to hold back something for the evening. The eight o'clock show on Saturday night was usually my best because I was completely warmed up. Saturday night is supposed to be the night you burn it up, and I did. I was always tired before I hit the ice and usually had the feeling that it would either be the worst show of the week or the best. Somehow it was always the best.

That left me with Sunday, which was a two-show day. Sundays were tough too. In fact, the whole tour was tough. Being on the road and working that kind of wear-you-down schedule gives you a fair idea of how far you can push yourself. I learned a lot about my limits and capabilities in those years, about how to pace my energy, about how far to push. I think it revealed and helped bring forward a lot of character too. Instead of impressing the judges, I had to impress the crowd. This was a good thing for my skating, because the things the crowds responded to were the things that were important to the style of skating that I was developing.

In those early years I was still far from evolving what I would call my mature style. I needed time to do that, and I needed to grow away from my mother's dominating influence. While she supported my attempt to incorporate a balletic feel into my skating, she still reined me in when she felt that art was edging too far into sensuality. I had yet to come to the realization that expressing myself as a woman could not be done without sensuality, but inside I knew it. My skating, my sense of costumes, makeup, hair, lighting all were going in that direction. The reaction of the crowds told me that it was right . . . or at least right for me. It wasn't until midway through my career in the ice shows that my style matured in that expressive way that became my trademark.

The one event that helped me to grow beyond my mother's vision was becoming a mother myself. Having my first son, Andy, changed me. It changed my skating. It changed my marriage. It changed everything. But I skated for nearly eight years in the ice shows before Andy and another seven or eight after Andy. In those first seven years I put together the elements that would eventually become my style. One of the biggest tricks—doing nothing at the right time—was something I picked up from an unlikely source.

A key lesson for any performer is how to hold an audience's attention. I learned my lesson not from a high-strung diva or a prima ballerina, but from an ice clown named Mr. Frick. He was an old-fashioned clown—just like in the circus—only he did his pratfalls on the ice. He had been half of a team called Frick and Frack, but Frack, who was not in good health, had retired. So Mr. Frick had the comic relief chores all to himself in Ice Follies.

The way the show was paced, I usually followed him. I would be backstage, a big bundle of nerves, anxious to get out on the ice; but there was no such thing as getting out in a hurry when Mr. Frick was exiting. When it came to milking the audience for applause, this guy could have had his own dairy. When he was finished with his act, they would announce his name and he would exit very slowly, as if he couldn't see how to get off. Believe me, he knew his way off. While he was "lost in the spotlights," which happened conveniently just as his applause started, he would stop and stand there, acting as if he had never heard so much applause before, which of course would goad the audience into giving him even *more* applause. I learned a great lesson from Mr. Frick: A performer can move an audience by doing nothing. You don't have to keep moving and bowing. Sometimes just standing there and letting the applause wash over you relaxes the audience and makes them even more generous in their response. Carlo thought I never knew how to take bows properly. He was right, but even the great, classy, and continental Carlo was not able to teach me to take a bow. It took a baggy-pants comedian with great crowd-sense to teach me that just standing there can be gracious.

After nearly a half dozen years of performing in other people's shows, in 1973 Bob Banner suggested that I put together my own show, a two-hour review with some comedy, some musical acts, and a lot of skating. Bob used his show biz connections to convince Bill Harrah to let him produce the show at Harrah's Casino in Lake Tahoe. Skating as the headliner in my own show seemed like a terrific idea, so Mom, Greg, and I talked it over and we took the plunge.

Bill Harrah treated me like a bona-fide star. We were given a palatial house overlooking the lake. Even more than the cooks and maids and the Rolls Royce that Harrah's gave us when we were in town, what I remember most was the electronic drapes. It was just like in one of those super bachelor pads in an early James Bond movie: You pressed a button and the drapes opened, revealing a beautiful view of Lake Tahoe.

The show itself was two hours and included dinner and cocktails—a kind of "Peggy's Dinner Theatre on Ice." But instead of being just the act at the top of the bill I was also the host of the show. That meant I had to welcome the crowd and—*gulp*—talk to them! I was very nervous about this. Up to that point I had basically let my skating talk for me, but now I had to get up there and say actual words.

"Don't worry. You can do it easily," Bob Banner said, being a good producer and trying to encourage the talent. "You skate a number first, then you say a few words of introduction, and then you introduce the next act, which performs while you change costumes for the next number."

As he always did, Bob calmed me down, at least for the moment. But no sooner had I left him than I began to obsess on how much was on my plate: *"I have all this choreography to remember plus all these lines. How am I going to remember it all?"*

My solution? I wrote my little script on my hand before I went out and skated. The skating was easy, but I was sweating bullets the whole time about having to talk to the audience.

I finished my number and picked up the microphone to address the crowd. It got very quiet. I looked down at my hand, and I couldn't read a thing! You see, I had written the script very tiny, so when the bright spotlights were glaring it was more or less invisible. Instead of freaking out, I basically confessed to the audience that I couldn't read the teeny letters I had written on my hand and that I was new at this hosting thing. I said I remembered that I was supposed to welcome them and talk about the acts and what a fun night it was going to be. I just winged it from there, and the audience got on my side. We all laughed and the show went on, and it was never that hard for me again. I realized that in entertainment people are looking for you to do well. It is not like skating, where judges are looking for the things you mess up. But as far as my skating was concerned, it might just as well have been judges in the audience. For that whole engagement, five weeks and seven days a week, I never missed one move. I landed every jump and every spin just the way I tried to do it for Carlo when I was training for competition.

If you are honest with your effort, audiences can be very forgiving. They were that way in Tahoe, and they were the same when we took Peggy Fleming's Concert on Ice on the road. We played a lot of theatres-in-the-round, which was an intimate departure from the Ice Capades arena shows and more like the family feeling of our show at Harrah's. Some towns that wanted us didn't have a theater-in-the-round, so we would end up in a tent or a venue with a roof and open-air sides.

The only difference from city to city was where I would make my entrance for the big number, which was *Swan Lake*. One night we were playing in one of those places with open-air sides. The rehearsal in the afternoon was a breeze, and by that time in the tour we could have done the show in our sleep. What we hadn't counted on was that between the rehearsal in the afternoon and the show at night, they had decided to close the flaps on the sides. This complicated my entrance because the way *Swan Lake* started was that my partner first entered and skated around solo, then, on cue, I would enter from one of the aisles and join him. With the tent flaps down, I couldn't see very well, so there I was in the rear, peering through the flap, looking for the one aisle that allowed me to enter on the ice. The music was playing, and my partner, Paul Sibley, was gamely doing his best pretending he was supposed to be doing an extended solo before I showed up, but pretty soon the audience caught on that he was faking it. Finally, I found the right aisle and made it onto the ice. Even though it was a "serious" number, the audience was laughing. I was laughing. Paul was laughing. It's hard to be artistic under those circumstances. So Paul and I improvised for a while until we could keep a straight face, and then we got into the serious part of the piece. It was every performer's nightmare, only I lived it.

One of the reasons I had success in the ice shows—and success equals selling tickets—is that I loved the pieces that I skated and I was able to transmit that feeling to the audience. Just because you love something doesn't mean it's going to be great every time, unless you work at it. Like sex and marriage: Things that are lyrical, pleasurable, and emotional are things you have to work at to keep interesting.

Some nights I would be totally into the meaning of the lyrics of my songs. Some nights I would be into the feel and the flow of the costume. Some nights I would feel sensual energy from performing to a piece of music, which is not surprising, given that I skated to a lot of love songs. Whenever I felt that way, I would look out from behind the curtain and pick out some guy who looked interesting and sexy. When I skated the number, I skated it to him, or at least with him in mind. I would let myself go into a fantasy with that stranger. When I was on the ice, in the lights, with the music and the motion, there was a certain kind of flirtation that gave great energy and expressiveness to my performance. The best part was, it was safe! I didn't even have to go for a cup of coffee with the guy . . . or even know his name. Sex with a proper stranger—in my fantasies—saved many a boring night on the ice.

Of course, sometimes with fantasies, as with the real thing, you just don't "feel like it." But when there are five thousand people spending their hard-earned dollars to be entertained, you have to find a way to "get up" for your performance. A little silliness can sometimes be just the ticket.

Robin Cousins and I skated together very well. He is an unbelievable skater. He has a tall thin body type that looks spectacular on the ice. There is an airiness to his jumps that makes them look twice as big and effortless at the same time. He also is very inventive and did a lot of his own choreography. When the moves come from within you, like they do with Robin, they are just that much more real.

Once Robin, Toller Cranston, and I performed together at Radio City Music Hall. Robin and I had this one scene that starts as a Currier and Ives kind of skating tableau. One of the young boys is taken with one of the girls. He falls asleep in the sleigh and he dreams what it will be like when he grows up and can skate with her. Robin was the grown-up boy, and I was the grown-up girl. We were supposed to be head over heels in love with each other as we skated a deeply romantic duet.

Sounds nice, but the problem was, we didn't feel that romantic about the piece. We did, however, like to play jokes on each other, little practical jokes. They would always come out of left field, but when they did, we couldn't lose our composure or even crack a smile. That was the energy that gave life to the piece—we were trying our level best to get through it without bursting into laughter.

One day we got to the part where we skate toward each other with deep longing. I closed my eyes and skated toward Robin. I had my friend, Jean, write something on my eyelids that I knew would get him. As I got closer to Robin, he couldn't hold in his laughter as he read the words on the closed eyelids of his "beloved":

BITE ME, the writing said.

Robin came right back at me the next performance. I had to do a quick change from my little skating outfit into a long Currier and Ives turn-of-the-century-era coat. I didn't have time to think. I just had to get into the coat and get back on the ice. As I moved into the spotlight, I could see Robin's revenge. He had connived with the wardrobe person to insert padding in the chest of the coat so that I looked like I had humongous breasts. I couldn't even see my feet. Once I was out there on the ice, there was nothing to do about it but to finish the piece while trying my best to keep a straight face.

The taste level never recovered after that. In fact, it kept descending, but we were having such fun one-upping each other that I think we skated rather well. I know this makes us sound like airheaded kids—but a little airheadedness is sometimes just what the doctor ordered. As I said, anything to keep it interesting.

The fun and fantasies of life on the road were a world apart from the suburban mom life that I began to live after Andy was born on January 30, 1977. Diapers, baby food, two A.M. feedings: If I ever needed a reality check after all that show biz, Andy was it. I was tired all the time but so in love with this baby that it was worth it.

I couldn't bear to be away from Andy, but my career required me to travel, so I just packed him up and took him on the road with me. It made life more complicated, but it was better than being separated from him. If that had happened I might have given up skating right then. When my second child, Todd, came along, I had a less demanding road schedule so I didn't feel the same need to take him on the road everywhere I went.

But Andy was my first, and I was learning the rules on-the-fly. I was also completely nervous and anxious about every little thing, which is par for the course with first-time moms. I would bundle him up, and the next time I checked on him he would have kicked the covers off. I started putting two pairs of pajamas on him, secure in the belief that at least he wouldn't get cold during the night. Of course, it turned out that I bundled him up so much that he got heat rash, completely ignoring the advice of my husband—who is a dermatologist and knows a thing or two about rashes.

I wasn't the only one getting a crash course in mothering while skating in an ice show. Susie Berens, my skating friend from those early-morning sessions when my dad ran the Zamboni in Pasadena, was also a new mom and a member of our skating troupe. She took her baby, Mark, with her too, so we had a little traveling nursery in the middle of the Ice Follies. We shared sitters, and we got connecting rooms, which made it easy for the kids to visit and play as they got older.

By the time Andy was ready to go to school I had gotten over my separation anxiety. I also cut back on my show schedule and started to go on shorter tours, while Andy stayed home with Greg. Andy pretty much forgot about all the times he saw me skate when he was little. I had him join me during school vacation when he was fifteen or so. Todd was just a toddler then and I also had him along for a week or two, but I brought him separately from Andy, so that each of my children would get some special attention.

Andy hadn't seen me skate in front of an audience since he was a little boy. I came out toward the end of the show in white chiffon and did a beautiful number, after which the crowd gave me a standing ovation. For an encore I put on a hat and a pair of sunglasses and did something funny and funky. The tune, a big hit at the time, was "Ice Ice Baby" by Vanilla Ice, and there was an even bigger standing ovation. No standing ovation could make a mother feel as good as what happened when I went back to the dressing room.

Andy yelled in, "Mom, you *ruled!*" I don't care if they give me a ticker tape parade down Broadway, I could never dream of feeling more gratified.

5

The View from the Booth

By the late 1970s I had been traveling and skating for almost twenty years. I was beginning to feel that my skating schedule was taking me away from home too much in the most important years for my family, and I was ready for something new in my Long Program. My next opportunity, becoming a network commentator, gave me the chance to earn good money doing something new and challenging, but it didn't require me to be away as much. It also let me have a front row seat to some of the greatest moments in skating over the next twenty years.

I was ready for something new. The question was, of course, was America ready for me with a mike in my hand?

I had already tried it once. In 1972, while I was still doing my NBC specials and skating a heavy ice show schedule, NBC asked me to be an on-camera commentator for their Olympic coverage in Sapporo. Three years before *Saturday Night Live* invented the "Not Ready for Prime Time Players,"

I earned that title. I hardly knew which end of the microphone was up. NBC basically threw me out there with Jim Simpson, a nice classy guy whose lack of knowledge about skating equaled my lack of knowledge about commentating. We were a perfectly awful team. The folks at ABC must not have seen my work when they asked me to be an on-camera personality eight years later.

I had my audition in 1980. Nobody told me it was an audition at the time, and they haven't confirmed it to this day, but I have always had a feeling that it was my tryout. I was in Lake Placid to perform a special exhibition piece for ABC. They were doing a program on American skating, and they invited Dorothy Hamill and me to perform. We spent a whole day taping our show in the arena, and for a few hours, I was back in that wonderful feeling that I had on my NBC specials: a great crew, the best technical equipment in the world, and the ice all to myself. It was shot beautifully by the director, Doug Wilson, whose work behind the camera was groundbreaking in capturing the movement and the feel of great skating. Doug was the guy who first figured out how to get those fluid moving shots on the ice where the camera moves as smoothly as the skater: He put a cameraman in a wheelchair and had a skater push the chair around the ice. No fancy gear, no high-tech anything, just a wheelchair and an ice skater, but it worked.

When we arrived in Lake Placid, ABC's voice of the Olympics, Jim McKay, interviewed me about the upcoming competition among a field of women that included the favorites, Lisa-Marie Allen and Linda Fratianne. They also asked Dorothy Hamill the same questions. Years later, when I look at the tapes of that day, I can see that, ever so subtly, Jim was asking things in such a way that we would give the kinds of answers commentators give. I was very easy and loose on that day, and I spoke from the heart and didn't think too much beyond that. Television likes that. Less than a year later I was offered the job as ABC's skating commentator working alongside Dick Button. Everything seemed perfect except for one thing: I felt Dick Button didn't like me.

It had all started when Dick was commenting on some of my amateur competitions. Ever the perfectionist, Dick would pick up on a few less-than-perfect things in my performance, and my mom decided that Dick was against me and for my competitors, whether it was Tina Noyes or Janet Lynn or whoever. Mom was supersensitive—make that super supersensitive—when it came to criticism of my skating. Dick henceforth was in her doghouse.

At that time I was accustomed to letting Mom and my coaches tell me what to think. I had enough on my mind with my skating. So when Mom said Dick didn't like me I said, "Okay, Mom."

Before I go too much further into my saga with Dick, I must tell you about the first story I heard about him. Now, no one ever had a hard time telling Dick and me apart on camera: I'm the one with hair. These days Dick is very comfortable as a balding guy, but back in 1963, when I first met him, he was still wearing a toupee—even when he skated.

Once while Dick was demonstrating a move for ABC coverage, I was told he was skating very well and doing some awesome jumps. But right in the middle of something very fast and very difficult his toupee came undone. Rather than being crushed and embarrassed—even he would later admit it was funny—Dick just carried on with grace and style.

I thought then, and still think, this is a man with class.

I carried that positive image of Dick buried somewhere inside of me, but Mom's misgivings were uppermost. A few years later in 1966, when I was clearly the skater that the country had its eyes on, Dick began to interview me just as I came off the ice. These days you pretty much expect that to happen, but that was a new, in-your-face kind of broadcasting style back then. It all had to do with Roone Arledge's concept of making all sports coverage immediate and up-close. Roone was the moving force behind making ABC sports the Olympic Network, and he also created *Wide World of Sports* and *Monday Night Football.*

Dick was just doing his job, but I didn't like it. I was still shy and very intimidated by all the lights and cameras. I also felt very vulnerable when I came off the ice. Since Mom had already planted these seeds of mistrust about Dick, I took his direct questioning as another example of his not being fond of me.

And so I carried that emotional baggage about Dick around for years. Think about yourself in high school. Remember how much any little slight seemed to hurt so much? Well, I was a high school girl when I experienced what I perceived as Dick's slights.

At first, when I took the ABC job, Dick and I kind of kept our distance. Basically, I was intimidated by him. He was so well spoken and I felt rather clueless. I watched Jim McKay and his way of doing things, and I paid close attention to Dick. I tried to do as much homework as I could, but this wasn't a high school exam. It was two people doing something togeth-er. It was like being a young girl on the dance floor with a mas-ter of ballroom dancing. He knew how to lead, but I had trouble knowing how to follow. Complicating matters was the fact that we were both perfectionists and skaters, and we tried to be perfect in our commentary. I have since learned, and so has Dick, that the audience is not looking for perfection in commentators; they are looking for some insight from a believable human being. Natural conversation is almost as important as knowing your subject.

But that took years. In the beginning, there was a lot of tension. Only part of it was the newness on the job. The other part was the emotional baggage I had with Dick. Then one day Jean Hall, my assistant and probably my closest friend, was helping me organize my old videos, including the ones of the performances at which Mom felt that Dick had got on my case.

"Hey, Peggy," Jean said, "did you ever listen to the old tapes of Dick? You know, the ones when your mom thought he was criticizing you?"

"Actually, I don't think I ever did."

"Well, you should. I think you're in for a surprise."

I looked and listened to those tapes with adult ears, and I was shocked. Dick Button had actually *liked* my skating. He said wonderful things about me and did so consistently. Mom, ever protective, took it as a slight if he was even moderately critical of me—or if he moderately praised another skater. It turned out that Mom, with the best of intentions, had been sensitive to slights that were never there.

There's nothing like knowing you have been unfair to someone to make you feel horrible. I had to talk to Dick. The very next time I had an opportunity, I sat down with Dick in a quiet moment after an event and told him what I had been carrying around all these years.

I didn't hem and haw. Instead I took a deep breath and said, "Dick, I don't know if you're aware of this, but I had bad feelings about you all through my competitive career. I always thought you didn't like me, and my mom told me to be careful around you. She didn't trust you. It all had to do with your commentary on my skating, but I've looked at the old tapes, and now that I don't have Mom interpreting them for me, I see that I was wrong. That explains why I may have been standoffish and a little cool when we work together."

Dick was flabbergasted, absolutely horrified. "I always admired your skating—and your mom, honestly. I've always said you added a lot to the sport. I don't know how your mom could have had those feelings."

"It probably had more to do with her problems and insecurities than anything you said," I answered.

That was probably the best and certainly the most important discussion I have had in my broadcasting career. Dick has since become one of the special people that I feel close to. All you have to do is look at the photo on his ABC credentials: Instead of the usual professional mug shot that most of us carry, he always drags me into the picture with him and I oblige with something mature like sticking two fingers behind his head in a donkey-ears V. We are just big kids at heart, which—even though you don't see that part of us on camera—is one of the reasons we come across as a believable team.

I know we're a good team, because we wouldn't have lasted so long—nearly twenty years—if we weren't; you would see it when we are together on camera. You can't fool audiences. They know when a team doesn't click and when one does, like Matt Lauer and Katie Couric. Good chemistry is something you can't define, but you sure know it when you see it.

To me, one of the most valuable parts of my friendship with Dick is off camera. He is a great traveling companion. He knows so much history and art and culture, and he's made our trips together more memorable than just a series of hotel rooms and arenas with a lot of air travel in between. I have learned by hanging out with Dick, and he's been somewhat of a father figure for me—although the older we get, the less far apart in age we seem to be.

I think this side of Dick comes out in his work as a commentator. We are on the same page in our view of skating but we are not the same person. Call it the mom in me, but I tend to be more gentle in my criticism than Dick is. Where Dick will always have a comment on a jump or a spin, I am just as likely to think about how things work with the music, and the costumes. Dick will rarely talk about the costumes (unless, of course, they're really really bad).

Dick likes great skating, and he's quick to point out when somebody falls short of the mark. I am not so quick on the trigger. I am always aware that these are kids out there. Coming from a not very privileged background, I'm always sensitive to the struggles that these competitors go through off the ice and the struggles of families that make big financial sacrifices for their kids. It's the world I came from. I am hypersensitive to the feelings of the competitors, especially when they don't do as well as they had hoped.

That explains why I hate having to hold the microphone in the "kiss and cry" area almost as much as I used to dislike it when commentators came up to me in my skating days. It's just part of modern television, and I guess the viewer gets something out of understanding how the skater sees his or her performance, but I sure hate sticking the mike in their faces and asking, "What went wrong?" at a time when they probably just want to run and hide. I remember when Michelle Kwan messed up at the 1997 Nationals—only a year before the 1998 Nationals, where she skated one of the greatest routines I have ever seen—she looked like she was going through torture.

We have all had this "joy of victory and agony of defeat" idea drilled into us about the Olympics. True enough, but I think it's important to point out that skating—make that any sport—has to be fun. As life goes on, I think it's reasonable to look for the fun in everything: It's what makes work, or exercising, or any of life's chores easier to handle. Being on the road with ABC has been a lot of work, but there has also been a fair amount of fun in between the pressure cooker appearances, even at the grandmother of all television events...the Olympics.

When I recall Sarajevo, I don't think of Yugoslavia today, a country full of war and sadness. I think of a gorgeous city ringed by mountains, filled with beautiful, hopeful young athletes. I think of Katarina Witt in a ravishing costume, ushering in an era of glamour in the Olympics, and Scott Hamilton skating so beautifully. Scott—with his high spirits, his energetic skating, his being adopted and overcoming a childhood disease that led to a growth deficiency—I don't think there was ever an Olympic champion who reminded us of so much of the joy of the sport and the joy of life.

From those same games, I think of Torvill and Dean's evocative, seductive, lyrical, passionate free dance to *Boléro*. The choice of music was a breakthrough. Rather than relying on a number of pieces for changes in tempo, style, and feel, they went with one piece that captivated your attention as a whole. Apart from their musical adventurousness, they pushed the envelope of the rules when it came to their delightful lifts and the sensuous intertwining of legs and arms in their breathtaking choreography. There are very few "wow!" performances that set a new course for a sport. In the dance event, I think that one did, and I am glad I was there to see it.

When I remember Sarajevo, I also recall our crew hotel—stuck in the middle of nowhere. There was nothing nearby, so we became very faithful regulars at the restaurant and bar. Greg was able to get away and spend time with me, for which I was very grateful. One night we tried to have a nice quiet dinner, which is a near impossibility when you are on the road with a TV crew. As it did every night, our table grew and grew as more and more friends and colleagues showed up. Somehow every meal became family style and the last one to arrive would be stealing French fries from the early birds. On that night John Denver, who was in town to see the games and to do musical pieces for the broadcast, came in with his guitar. John was a folk singer in the old tradition—he knew just about every song ever sung. He had the most beautiful clear voice and you couldn't help but join in—whether it was "Up on Cripple Creek" or "All Shook Up." Song after song, we stayed around the table until two A.M. As the games wore on, John's song festival became a regular occurrence. It's not such a bad way to spend your time—watching great athletes at work and winding down with your own private John Denver concert.

Of course, for every John Denver folk festival, there are probably ten stories of blowing off steam in a less than mature way. Sometimes when I am on the road I wonder: Did we ever get out of high school? Olympic trainees often miss most of the partying part of high school, and they make up for lost time at the Olympics. One incident that has gone down in the Peggy Fleming/ABC Sports Road Show Hall of Fame is the party in my bed in Orlando—which sounds a lot more titillating than it was.

I had just started traveling with Jean Hall, who wasn't my assistant yet, just a buddy on the road. As a flight attendant for American Airlines, Jean had some flexibility in her schedule and could meet me in different cities. I needed a buddy because when you are on the road, everybody has a job to do and, if you are on-camera talent, then you end up being alone with your notes and videotapes a lot of the time. As a former apprentice with the Harkness Ballet and a fun person, Jean shares my taste in many things. She has turned out to be one of the reasons I've been able to keep up a life with so much travel.

Jean and I were in Orlando for the 1992 Nationals, and it went late and we didn't get back to the hotel until nearly midnight. We stopped in to the restaurant for a bite and a glass of wine and, just like Sarajevo, our table grew to four, then to ten, then to twenty. We stayed until closing time and headed for our rooms. Since we were all on the same floor it quickly became a dorm party. I was in my room when Julie Moran (who was the host of ABC's figure skating coverage) in her pajamas, came over with her husband, Rob. Next came Curt Gowdy Jr. (our producer) and Jimmy Roberts, a commentator for ESPN, then many others. We started getting into the snacks in our mini-bars and pretty soon most of the floor was at our party, on my king-sized bed, making quite a commotion. Somebody must have complained about the noise, because soon after, a big burly cop showed up. His name was Big John —no kidding.

Even when you have a lot of company, having a large police officer come into your bedroom at two-thirty in the morning is a bit unsettling. I felt like the kid who was having a party at her house when her parents were supposedly away for the weekend. Big John stepped into the room, looked us over, and broke into a big smile.

"Hey, you're Peggy Fleming," he said.

I admitted it.

"I'm a fan of yours. Do you suppose I could get a picture with you?" he said in the sweetest voice.

There we were thinking we were going to be cited for disturbing the peace, and I run into a 250-pound skating fan.

"Sign it 'To Big John,'" he asked politely.

I gave him my autograph, and we toned our party down a little.

We party hard partly because when you are making television shows, the work is so intense. When we have a televised event coming up—currently we do about ten to fifteen a year, compared to three or four per year when I started—I study the routines until I know them pretty well. Often a skater performs the same routine at several competitions during a year so I have the chance to study the program and the jumps.

Watching so much skating, in contrast to working on my own skating, was an eye opener. I had been out of competition for more than a decade when I became a broadcaster. It helped me learn about myself as a person and a skater. It helped me shape my own style. The best thing about the pro circuit is that you get to skate plenty, but no one is keeping score. For the kind of skater that I am, one who is more interested in giving her heart and soul to a performance than in rewriting the record book, commenting was the ideal thing. Nowadays, we've brought competition into the pros, and I think it helped sharpen some skills. It's added some more jumps to the repertoire of skaters who would otherwise not have advanced athletically beyond what they did in their amateur careers. But in 1980, when I became a broadcaster, I hadn't been paying super close attention to what was going on in the amateur world. I was too busy doing two and three shows a day.

I was amazed at the changes that the years had wrought in the sport, both good and bad. I remember being very impressed by Denise Beillmann, a gifted athlete who maintained a lithe, feminine look. You may have heard broadcasters mention the Beillmann Spin, a move that Denise didn't invent, but which she popularized. It's a very pretty spin where you grab your leg from behind and put it over your head. I have tried it a few times and I'm not even close. Denise had the flexibility of a young gymnast.

I remember watching Denise land a triple lutz, the first woman ever to have accomplished that. Both Dick and I were very impressed. The young women skating today have trained and acquired athletic skills that go way beyond our training methods and skills in the late sixties—a phenomenon that is true in all sports. Inevitably, though, a sport comes to a time when a new move upsets the balance of the sport and something has to be done. Although I don't closely follow every sport, my ABC colleagues tell me that this is true across the board. In baseball they narrowed the strike zone after Bob Gibson allowed fewer runs per game than anyone had done in decades. In football, the advent of the powerful and athletic defensive player caused the league to issue a flurry of rules designed to protect the quarterback. As this book goes to press, the National Basketball Association, in response to low scoring, is considering ways to open up the game to more crowd-pleasing scoring.

The adjustment in my sport came when an American skater named Elaine Zayak won the World competition on the basis of one jump, her triple toe loop. After placing twelfth in her school figures, she moved up to seventh on the basis of her short program, which was full of triple jumps. Then in her long program, she piled up the points by landing that same jump—the triple toe loop—over and over in her four-minute-long program. It was, to my mind, not what skating was about. There was no attention to expression—it was just the same jump over and over again. I left those Worlds with a bad taste in my mouth as a result of where the pressure of winning and competition was taking my sport. It was hard for me to be enthusiastic about it.

The powers that be—or the powers that were—in skating felt the same way and instituted the so-called Zayak Rule, which forbade skaters from trying the same jump more than once, unless they did it in a combination that would add difficulty and variety.

Running up the score was only symptomatic of a larger problem in the sport; the emphasis on winning. That may sound a little odd coming from someone who is a dyed-in-the-wool competitor, but I wanted to win because it said something about me as an athlete and a determined person. I had no idea of the ways in which winning can change your life, as mine did after the Olympic medal.

Today, the results of winning are huge and well known: You become a star, and you stand to make millions. There is unbelievable pressure on the young skaters and the handlers, coaches, and hangers-on who come with the territory. It is that win-at-all-costs mentality that led to the bizarre Tonya Harding/Nancy Kerrigan episode in Detroit in 1994.

Tonya came out of it as a villain, which I don't think she was. She just surrounded herself with the wrong people, starting with her husband and his thug friends. As a kid from a background not terribly unlike my own—parents without a whole lot of money who had to scramble to keep their very dedicated daughter in an expensive and demanding sport—I could relate to her. But my mother taught me that one of the most important things in life is choosing the right friends and listening to the right people. That's what landed me in a good place and what nearly destroyed Tonya.

Tonya, though her skating style was not out of the Peggy Fleming book, was a terrific athlete and an absolutely astounding jumper. As we say in the sport, she really "put some air" under her jumps. She also had a rebellious "I'm going to skate things my way" kind of attitude. I like some of that in a skater.

Dick and I were there, of course, in the rink, watching Nancy Kerrigan just before the competition for the National championships. Shortly after we left, Nancy was attacked by some guy. We later learned that the guy had been put up to it by Tonya's husband. No sooner had we arrived at our hotel than we heard the news that Nancy had been hurt so badly that she couldn't possibly skate.

At the time we all assumed—since we were in Detroit, which had a pretty rough reputation—that it had been some kind of mugging. ABC, taking no chances, said they wanted to make sure that no random violence befell their people. When I opened the door to my room the next morning, there was a very large African-American gentleman standing right by the doorway.

"Hello," I said.

He must have seen the surprise in my eyes. "Miss Fleming, I'm Tanner, your bodyguard."

I had never had an official personal bodyguard before. From the moment I left my room to the minute I returned, he was by my side. He was a really nice guy and I enjoyed his company, but I think skating, and all sports, could do with a lot less of the crazed obsession with winning that leads to bodyguard situations.

That same pressure brought out enormous reserves of grit and style in Nancy Kerrigan. Up until the time of the attack, she was an accomplished skater and physically quite beautiful, but she was inconsistent. To her great credit, she managed to fight her way back from her injury. Rising to the occasion, and focused in a way I hadn't seen her before, she gave an outstanding performance in the Olympics. She could easily have won the gold medal and no one would have thought the judges were terribly off base. But a wonderfully expressive Oksana Baiul took the gold by putting one extra jump at the end freeskate.

That was when the pressure got to Nancy, and she went from a graceful competitor to a very ungracious loser. When Oksana, overcome by emotion, cried tears of joy for a good long time, Nancy's body language was unmistakably disgusted, as if to say, "Hey, can we shut off the waterworks and just get on with it?" Nancy skated so well that night and looked so gorgeous in her dress, but I think she took away from a great moment for her when she got so antsy. Oksana cried her makeup off—and then she took the time to redo it before they awarded the medals. Hey, you don't win that many Olympic gold medals in your life; I'd want my makeup together too.

We didn't have the same kind of pressure when I won my medal, but that doesn't mean there was none. I experienced my share on the way to my National and World championships, and I learned how to handle it. When the gold medal came and with it the TV specials, the endorsements, the mega-fame of being the *Sports Illustrated* and *Life* magazine cover girl and the darling of the media, I had a lot coming at me all at once.

In 1976, Dorothy Hamill was in line for the Peggy Fleming slot, at least that's the way I saw things back then in the early seventies. I don't mean by that to say that she skated like me. Where I was concerned with adding emotion to the athleticism in my skating, Dorothy, in her years as an amateur, emphasized athleticism and a put-together wholesome look, more like Carol Heiss but with extra flare. When Dorothy was beginning to put her skating together she worked with both Carlo and Bob Paul. It was when she first came out to see Bob that my mom, who saw Dorothy as a real comer, invited her to stay with us in Sherman Oaks. I was doing a photo session for NBC, and at Mom's suggestion, we took Dorothy along so that she could get a feel for my world after the gold.

Dorothy was gifted and dedicated and skated outstandingly to win her Olympic gold medal. But where I had all those years as a world champion before my gold, the rush of triumph was new to her. By that time, 1976, the media circus around the woman's gold medal winner was in high gear. Dorothy was an instant superstar. I confess I felt a touch of sibling rivalry at this point. I was a little fearful that she would take over in my role—with endorsements, with TV, with everything.

What I didn't realize at the time was that America's appetite for celebrities is boundless. There was room for both of us and then some. Still, as someone who rocketed to the top in a hurry, I think she was a bit overwhelmed by how big a deal it was. She kind of got lost for a while in a more Hollywood world. I thank my lucky stars that I had a regular guy for a boyfriend and husband, who kept things grounded in the real world in those early years.

Of course Dorothy pulled things together for herself eventually, but when you are young, the pressure of competition and the flood of the media after you win is a lot to handle, and it takes its toll.

As a broadcaster, I am part of the media that creates a frenzy wherever it shows up. I always try to keep in mind that these are young kids, wide-eyed and as fresh in the world as I was, some of them like I was, a total babe in the woods. I try to tell it as I see it, but when things aren't going well, I say it in the most gentle way possible. I hope my criticisms help people become better skaters: I have been told that they do. But I have taken something from broadcasting as well and incorporated it in my skating. As a commentator, I am free to experience the performance as an expressive work without worrying about overanalyzing every jump and spin. I try to feel the totality of the skater and to communicate that to the audience. Every skater has a unique way of moving around the ice, and I studied and finally began to feel the unique quality and to appreciate and learn from skaters who came after me but who pursued the same artistic goals that I had set for myself.

Broadcasting helped my own skating enormously. In this respect I have been very fortunate. For most athletes, being a broadcaster is something you do after you retire from competition and "hang up your skates," so to speak. In skating, however, many of us have a longer skating life after we finish competition. That's the great thing about the professional side of our sport. We are no longer solely judged on technical grounds—technique is now taken for granted. We are judged on how we entertain as athletes and artists.

That suits me fine. It is in line with the way I have felt about skating since that first day with Dad in the fifties: Skating was a way for a shy tomboy to express herself. Now that I am not as shy and long past the tomboy stage, skating is still a form of expression. As I grew older, as I mastered the technique, I was able to spend more time and more effort on the expression. When I am skating I use music, costume, lighting, and most of all, my body, to tell a story.

It took me a long time to get comfortable with using my body to tell a story to fifteen thousand people in an arena. To do that, I grew away from, and finally lost, the two people who had the most to do with my successes: Mom and Carlo. But in the process of doing so I gained the confidence to be who I really am and to tell the world that through my skating.

6

Becoming Me

By the 1980s, I began to find my own look and style. Once I did that, I was in a comfort zone in which I seemed to just flow into my skating. Between the Olympics and the 1980s my skating evolved, but it was still not there yet. During those years, the sport evolved too: the technical side is probably more difficult today but the artistic and expressive side are always open for more exploration. It was in that early eighties period when skating was evolving so quickly that the choreography, the music, the costumes, and the overall approach of people who skated with my sensibility started to come from a much freer place. The sentiment that Dick expressed when Michelle Kwan skated her gorgeous program in the Nationals in Phildelphia in 1998 gave words to what I had been attempting to do as I defined my skating in the early eighties: "She transcends her technique," Dick said. "I can almost feel her heart when she skates." That's just what I have always sought to do.

I had always sought to put that inner quality of expression in my skating. In the beginning there were a just few of us, like the Protopopovs, and Janet Lynn. But as the times changed so did skating. I didn't feel as if I were the only one pursuing the artistic side of skating while so much of the skating world was obsessed with higher jumps, more spins, pushing the physical side of the sport at the expense of the art in it. As I watched and often worked with these kindred spirits, we collectively nudged skating into a freer place than it had been when I was first competing,

Toller Cranston, with whom I appeared a number of times, was a true original from day one. He was an artist who just happened to have chosen skating as a medium, and it wasn't his only one. Toller is also terrific off the ice, and I think the confidence he gained artistically from his paintings gave him the belief in himself to take that same expressiveness and flamboyance into his skating. I have always said that skating is a sport that reveals much about the person skating. If we are tentative, languid, aggressive, seductive, or brash, it always comes out in our skating. You can't hide it. In Toller's skating you could always see the free spirit and the strong stretched-out moves of modern dance. His movements were elegant but not feminine. They were one-of-a-kind movements that only said "Toller." I never met a skater who moved like him.

In the early eighties, I appeared on Toller's "Strawberry Ice" special on Canadian television. It was a different kind of show than the ones I had done after winning my medal. Toller's idea was to use the medium of television to take skating into a fantasy world through imaginative costumes, weird scenarios, and lots of special effects in postproduction. In this one scene I was supposed to be the "Undersea Queen." After I skated, they would put some effeects on the tape, and it would look like I was swimming underwater. Toller choreographed the scene, and I had to do moves that I had never tried before to enhance that illusion. We did the number. The music was that beautiful Chopin piece from the credits in *The Turning Point*. I always loved the movie and the music. I could relate to it, so it wasn't that much of a stretch to try and express myself to that score. I told myself, "It's different, but that is what I want to be anyway." It turned out to be one of my favorite numbers that I ever tried on television, a little out there, but that's what skating needed and still needs.

Then there's Robin Cousins—not a skater whose style you would think of in the same breath as mine. But we are soul mates in the sense that during the 1980s and into the '90s we tried to do something different and more expressive than the textbook skating of the past.

Everything Robin does is bigger when he is on the ice. I think of him as the Tommy Tune of skating. He is coordinated in a way that taller people rarely are, especially when it comes to making fast moves. He has an almost Fred Astaire-like way of making everything he does look comfortable, yet he has the mental toughness of a born competitor. He is so much himself and makes the world meet him on his terms. He and I share the drive to put our identities out there on the ice as if to say, "Here is the real me, folks."

If I speak of soul mates, though, the one who was closest to me in spirit as an artist and skater was, in many ways, John Curry. We first worked together in the late '70s and it was all to the good for my skating. He was probably one of the most talented skaters I have ever met. Because he had so much ballet background, John was really pure of line, and his technical ability for the jumps was excellent. They weren't huge jumps, but they were technically perfect, and he landed in perfect positions and made them look effortless. His flare was intense but subtle. Apart from his technique, he had an ability to lose himself in his own world on the ice and, more important as an artist, he brought the audience into that world.

I miss John so much. AIDS has taken so many great artists from us, and skating never lost a bigger one, at the top of his form, than it did when John Curry died.

Working with John Curry helped me to put more of the feel and techniques of ballet into my skating. I always wanted my skating to look lyrical, connected to my inner feelings, and, most of all, feminine. I felt that was missing in the sport when I started. But I never wanted it to be all fluff and ruffles and pink bows. My skating had to show both gracefulness and strength, so in looking at ballet I always kept an eye out for moves and techniques that accomplished both of those goals. I also realized that clothing can help enhance a strong yet feminine effect.

I learned a good deal about the direction I wanted to take my clothing from being around ballet dancers. Cynthia Gregory, a prima ballerina with the American Ballet Theater, was one of the ballet stars who helped introduce me to this world. I first met Cynthia through her pictures, actually.

About twenty-five years ago Bil Leidersdorf, showed me some photos he had taken of Cynthia Gregory. They were quite lovely. He asked if I would come by his studio to sit for some photographs. I didn't know it at the time but Bil was a well-known performing arts photographer who studied under the great Martha Swope. Still, going to a photographer's studio in New York City was definitely among the things my mom might have thought twice about. So I didn't tell her. When I got to the studio, his fiancée, Jean Hall, was there, so I relaxed because there was another woman there. That was the first time I met Jean.

My reaction to the photos of Cynthia led to Jean's introducing us, and Cynthia and I became friends. I went to ballet rehearsals and performances, and the dancers came to my shows. We talked about music, movement, clothes—things that we had in common as artists and performers.

I loved the way that dancers used fabric to enhance their movements. Fabric had always been an underutilized element in skating, although that is changing now. Back then, however, it was just form-fitting little outfits with very little stretch, and coiffure with lots and lots of hair spray—what they used to call "helmet hair." These were things that worked against enhancing the motion of your body.

I particularly liked the rehearsal skirts that ballerinas wore, which gave such an elegant line to their moves. With our short skating dresses, all that people looked at were our legs. A flowing skirt seemed to work with my style of skating. Motion and line are the soul of skating.

I started to wear a ballet rehearsal skirt for my practice sessions, and soon I was making up moves that looked pretty with the fabric. I quickly learned that you have to take your fabric into account when you do your choreography. Different fabrics behave differently. If it has more weight to it will take a longer time for it to move—and to stop moving. You can do a turn or a spin, then stop, and the fabric will continue to wrap around you. To me, that is a look that builds excitement.

Chiffon—a material that I love and that I incorporated in those early years after the Olympics and before Andy—

behaves differently than the heavier fabrics. Because it is softer, you have to keep moving to make it behave more flatteringly. When I started wearing long chiffon skirts, like in the ballet, it was a real departure for skating. If they could do those moves in those dresses on the dance floor, I reasoned, I could put the fabric to the same kind of use in ice skating.

It did everything I wanted it to do. So many of the moves in skating happen so quickly that, unless you know the sport very well, you are going to miss them. The chiffon left a trail. It was a lingering continuation of the music and the flow. It also made me take my skating in a new direction. So much of the real business in skating comes as a result of the skater moving backward in preparation for a jump. Chiffon, though, wants to trail in back of you as you skate forward. It looks prettier when you are gliding and moving continuously, but it doesn't work so well when you do jumps and spins. Chiffon emphasizes the line and the flow, which is what I wanted my skating to be about. I began to skate moving forward more, which was more romantic, more lyrical. Like a sparkler that kids like to wave at a campfire so they can see its glowing trail and a continuous move in the dark, the clothes and fabric I used helped me build that illusion.

My interest in using clothing to enhance my style and my lines probably goes back to that chartreuse dress that I wore when I won my gold medal—but that was just a baby step. I really began to explore costumes when Bob Mackie designed my clothes on those first NBC specials. He was so talented that I rarely opened my mouth to express an opinion. I honestly didn't know how to speak up for myself yet: Skating, as far as the skater's thoughts and words go, is a silent sport. My mom had no trouble letting Bob know how she felt, though, and she did not want me looking too sexy. He was also new to skating and the demands and requirements it placed on the clothing designer. The result was beautiful work, but Bob definitely felt reined in. He created outfits that were more suited to a glamorous performer at a night club than to a gliding athlete. I sometimes felt overwhelmed by them.

From Bob Mackie I learned the importance of drama in clothing, of shining in the spotlight. When I next went to work with designer Pete Menefee, I began to take the steps that evolved into my own highly personal style. Pete had been a dancer, and he and I shared an impulse to explore a softer look as in ballet. We discovered how much we could do with a thin layer of chiffon. The costumes we came up with were light and airy, and full of motion, but they also expressed the strength and athleticism of the sport.

To my mind, the look I had been seeking finally came together in the costume that Pete Menefee designed for me to skate to Jane Oliver's "Some Enchanted Evening" in 1981. It had a beautiful white bodice, spaghetti straps, minimal beading, and a long chiffon skirt cut on the bias. It was a combination of the romantic, the lyrical, the lilting, and the dreamlike, all of it becoming a sensual languid mood: flowing, but outside of time somehow. To be in a dream while I skated and to invite others into that dream—that was what I had been trying to say with my skating since I was a little girl.

I also began to work with Jef Billings, assistant to Bob Mackie. Jef immersed himself in skating and has since become the biggest and most successful designer of professional skating costumes. Jef had a subtle feel, perfectly in tune with mine and does the greatest beadwork I have ever seen. For many years he made costumes for me that always looked rich and never glitzy.

I don't want to give the impression that my skating became one effortless and graceful glide as soon as I started using wispy fabrics. Though I was using fabric to express myself in my skating, at its most fundamental level, skating is a sport, and in all sports things can go wrong, as they did for me one horrific night in the summer of 1986.

It was the one hundredth anniversary of the Statue of Liberty. As part of the festivities, there was a showbiz and sports extravaganza out at the Meadowlands in New Jersey. A large number of top skaters and gymnasts were there. I was well into my new wispy look, aided by a long chiffon scarf that accentuated my moves. The wardrobe person, who thought she was just doing her job, took my scarf and suggested ironing the cloth. As an athlete, I had trained myself with unstarched, unironed fabric. My timing was all based on the way an unironed unslippery, unclinging scarf should have felt in my hand. Ironed fabric doesn't behave the same way and, hence, my timing was off.

I had finished one move and was about to begin another and hadn't taken this new behavior of my trusty old scarf into account. I caught my skate on the scarf and stumbled for what seemed like forever before a live television audience of millions. I wasn't alone that night. Dorothy Hamill took a similar spill, and she didn't have any assistance from the wardrobe department. But don't believe what they say about misery loving company: The two of us were terribly embarrassed. Still, that wasn't enough to put me off experimenting with fabrics. I felt from the first that Pete Menefee had a style that worked for me.

I knew I had finally achieved my look because it felt right for the music that moved me the most as a skater, those special songs that I could *feel* as I skated. Old favorites now had new life for me, like "Ave Maria" and Pachelbel's *Canon in D,* which was a particular favorite of Greg's.

Of course, no skater stays happy forever with one look, and as my style evolved, so did the costumes. Around 1990, or just about the time Nancy Kerrigan was coming up in the ranks, I was struck by her costumes and would mention them on the air, which was something I did only when I thought a costume was particularly beautiful. Vera Wang, who designed those clothes, had two things going for her: First, she was modern and expressive, and second, she had been a serious skater herself. She understood clothes, and she understood skating, which was a great combination.

After one of the broadcasts where I complimented her designs, Vera sent me the nicest thank-you note. Then, in 1998, I accepted an invitation to appear for a second time in a show called "Gershwin on Ice." I had always loved the music of George Gershwin and had skated in the show the previous year. No woman likes to wear the same dress at the same event more than once, so I wanted something completely new. I thought Vera was the right one, and I approached her.

Now when I say I wanted to have a sensual style, that doesn't mean I was ready for Vera to recreate the look she had used for Sharon Stone. The first things she showed me were very high fashion and see-through. I liked the idea though, so we went with a beige body stocking that gave the illusion of nude. Both dresses that she came up with were very body-oriented. They could cling and hang at the same time. For "Rhapsody in Blue" she created a midnight blue dress with a little bit of glitter and sheer sleeves. The dress for "Summertime" was kind of a stretchy oxblood crepe that wrapped around me. It was totally slinky, the kind of thing you would wear on a hot night in New Orleans. If I ever wanted to take a snapshot for the time capsule, I think it would be in one of those two dresses.

I am not done skating, but I do it less every year, and every year it seems to take longer to get in shape for a performance. Even though so much of my life on the ice was my struggle to define myself rather than just doing what Mom and Carlo said, liberating myself also had its costs. My supports are no longer there for me.

In 1991, the year before Mom died, I was preparing for a world tour, also semi-officially known as Champions on Ice or The Tom Collins Tour. Tom's a skater and promoter whom I first met when he managed Holiday on Ice. Bob Paul and I were working out a number, and Mom, who was in a wheelchair at the time, came down to watch. I was already well into my mature style of skating, but Mom still saw Little Peggy out there. "Be sure you include those little toe turns in the encore," she advised, "they always loved that."

"Oh, Mom!" I thought, "Here I am in my forties, and you are still putting in those moves from when I was a teenager."

I kept my thoughts to myself and, for that rehearsal, I put those moves in.

Mom was happy. Within a year she was gone. Without question she is the one person without whom I would not have become a skater. Her titanic temper, her enormous will, her fierce protection from anything she perceived as a threat or an attempt to exploit me, were like a suit of armor. She was my shield and my mom, and I loved her so very deeply. I had a hard time skating after I lost her. The same thing happened to me after Carlo died in 1997. Even if I didn't need or crave their criticism anymore, it still felt like something was missing. I didn't realize how much of a loss that was until I got back on the ice. Even as I write these words now, I find myself shedding tears. That emotion still washes over me whether I'm ready or not.

I wasn't at all ready when Carlo died. It was so sudden. Mom's decline was slow, and the end was anticipated, but Carlo died almost in front of me. I was covering the World championships at Lausanne, where one of Carlo's students, Nicole Bobek, was in the running. The night before he had his heart attack, he and I had walked up the hill to our hotel overlooking Lake Geneva. I remember he seemed a little out of breath. "Carlo," I said, "you have to do more walking and get in shape."

"I'm getting too old, Peggy," he answered. When we reached the hotel, Toller Cranston was in the entrance, and the three of us stood around talking for a while. We enjoyed catching up on good old times. Carlo was so funny that night and so . . . well, I guess the word is *cute*. I would never have said that to him, but his quick way of talking and his hand gestures and his courtly manners had always struck me as *cute*. We said good night, and that was the last time I spoke with him.

The next morning I was at the practice rink, and I caught sight of Carlo on his way to get a sandwich. After I left the building, he had his heart attack. I got back to the hotel a few hours later, and Meg Streeter—a producer from ABC who knew Carlo well—called to tell me what had happened, hoping in some way to cushion the blow that I would have felt if I first heard about it in the press. It was terribly considerate of her, but I was just devastated.

Because of my relationship with Carlo, ABC offered to have me come back to the rink to break the news on the air within the hour. I appreciated their offer, but there was no way I could compose myself. I told the network what I really needed to do was to find Christa, Carlo's wife. She was in their room at the hotel, and I was surprised how composed she was. I could see that she had been crying, but to outward appearances, she seemed more in control than I was.

She sat there with her suitcases all packed. "Are you getting ready to leave?" I asked.

"No," she said, "but I wanted to pack Carlo's things up. It was too upsetting to see them hanging in the closet." Their son, Lorenzo, had come in the night before to have dinner with his parents, so at least his mother wasn't alone. Christa and I embraced and cried, and seeing her helped me for the moment.

When I was by myself in my room, though, I felt the loss wash over me again. I cried all night. The next morning, I had to pull myself together and get ready to go to work. Again, Christa's example helped me get through it. Rather than leave the competition, she decided to stay there for Nicole. She was sure that was what Carlo would have wanted. "If Christa can pull herself together and be supportive of Nicole," I told myself, "I can go on the air." Carlo would surely have approved.

That evening was the climax of the championships—the women's finals. ABC was very patient and understanding. They said if I didn't feel I could make it through the announcement, I didn't have to, but it was something I wanted to do. "That's okay," I said. "Just be patient with me, and I'll get through it."

Right before I went on, Robin Cousins came into the dressing room and we talked. Robin and I are very close, and I could open up to him as he could to me. We both got very emotional, which only made it that much harder to go on camera.

Terry Gannon, our host, and Dick Button both knew what I was going through, and they were there for me too. I could only do short takes before the tears and emotions would overcome me. I remember doing one set-up to a comment about Carlo and just about dissolving before I got to the end. Terry saw how hard it was. When I finished—barely keeping my composure—Terry slid his arm around me and gave me a squeeze not visible to the camera. He too had been an athlete who lost his coach, the basketball genius Jim Valvano, to cancer, so he understood. It's hard for me to express the deep relationship between a coach and a skater. It is a bond that is unique.

After the competition was over, on the morning of the exhibition, there was a memorial service at the headquarters of the Olympic Committee. Dick Button hosted it. It was a nice event, full of life, not down and sad. Everyone who spoke had so many fun stories to tell. Meg put together a film clip of Carlo teaching—Carlo with the wild gestures, the face of a thousand expressions. Juan Antonio Samaranch, the President of the International Olympic Committee, gave an Olympic flag to Christa.

Then came my turn. I still have a copy of that speech. It was a good-bye to my coach and also, in a way, to my mom.

This is so hard for all of us, but what's helped me get through this week has been the strength I've seen in

Christa. It's the same strength that Carlo tried to instill in all his skaters—skaters who were lucky to be working with a man of legendary coaching skills, compassion, and a great sense of humor.

Just as Carlo was a skating legend, my late mother in her own way was also a legend in figure skating. She sat through every one of my practices, analyzing how things were progressing, and at the end of every day, Carlo could expect that inevitable phone call from her. The minute he walked through the door that phone would ring and Carlo would find a comfortable chair. Some evenings, because he knew it would be at least an hour's conversation, Christa would serve him dinner while my mother discussed the day's practice.

I am sure the minute Carlo got to Heaven, that phone began to ring.

He loved and understood this sport so well that his talent and his patience never wavered, for me, for my mother, for John, for Dorothy, for Robin, for Nicole.

I've come full circle with Carlo in this beautiful country. He brought me my first world title in Switzerland. He introduced me to my dear husband, Greg, in Switzerland. And now he's left us in Switzerland.

The night before he died, we walked up the hill to our hotel together, talking about the competition and about the future of skating. After a few minutes' climb, Carlo stopped me, puffing and laughing and said, "Peggy, it's too fast, too fast!"

And that's what I feel like his time with me was:

Too fast. Too fast.

Later that year, in August 1997, we held a tribute to Carlo at Lake Arrowhead. Paul Wylie, Dorothy Hamill, Caryn Kadavy, Robin Cousins, and Nicole Bobek all skated. Again the emotions started to well up. Even little Todd, who came with Greg and me, could sense it.

"Are you nervous, Mommy?" he asked.

"Maybe a little. I want this to be perfect for Carlo," I answered.

"Carlo will be there to help you get through it," Todd said, as if he really knew that were true.

That night there were tables set for dinner on the ice and a clear space for skaters. When I came out, Todd stood on his chair. He didn't budge through my whole performance of "Ave Maria." When I finished, he clapped harder than any fifty-two-pound boy ever clapped.

He had never seen me skate in front of a crowd before.

The great thing about that tribute was how well everybody skated: every single one of us. That was a rarity. I remember every skater coming off the ice and saying, "That's the best I have skated in years."

Joy, sadness, emptiness, love—a lot of emotions were there. Mom is gone. Carlo is gone. But my children are here. Most of all, there is the one person I have leaned on since I was a girl, and he is still there for me.

Greg.

7

Being a Mom

or many people, the thing that finally makes us grow up is becoming a parent. It was certainly true in my case. Before our children came along, Greg and I had spent seven years during which I did the ice shows while he became a physician. We had more money than I had ever had before, and we spent most of it wisely, but a decent amount of it went to having fun: my first Porsche, our town house in San Francisco, nice clothes. I was living out the dreams of a young girl who grew up having to do without. Even though I was enjoying being an adult, I was still very much my mother's daughter, which meant that even when I was an adult, she maintained a lot of the psychological influence that she had had over me when I was a young skater.

Babies changed everything, for the better.

Some people seem to get pregnant just like that. For me it wasn't that easy. After a lot of trying, I started to think that maybe I couldn't get pregnant. Maybe all that skating had done something to my body. My girlfriends reassured me. "Relax," they would say, "it takes time. Sometimes you try too hard. Somehow things just happen when you relax and don't think about it."

I relaxed, but being a modern woman who read magazines like *Glamour,* I also had my thermometer out and I knew what day of the month I was ovulating. Whenever that was, we did our job, whether we wanted to or not. Grueling work, but Greg rallied like a true champion.

It was during that trying-hard-but-pretending-I-wasn't-trying time that my friend Martha Neumann called. Martha and I have been close friends since Greg and Martha's husband, Kurt, were internal medicine residents in the early 1970s. Martha, who was a big believer in the relaxed school of getting pregnant, offered to have her young son Jake stay with us for a few days. She thought it would help Greg and me get used to the idea of parenting if we actually saw what a real, live child was like at home.

Jake was two years old at the time and a really sweet little boy. When Martha told us her idea, we thought it sounded great. Then he showed up. After Martha left, Greg and I looked at each other with the same thought: "What do you do with a two-year-old?" We really hadn't thought it through, and having gone through that weekend, I say, "Thank God they don't come out of your body as two-year-olds. It's much better if everybody has some time to get used to what they're supposed to do." No sooner had Martha and Kurt left for the weekend then we had a panic attack because we had a swimming pool without a fence around it. If it would have done any good I would have drained it right there, but I realized then that Jake could fall into an empty pool and hit his head on the concrete! Parenting, it became apparent to me, brings a whole new level of worrying.

"You know, Greg," I said, "Martha and Kurt are very brave to trust us with Jake."

I had to do some grocery shopping, so I took Jake to the supermarket and popped him in the shopping cart. We cruised up and down the aisles and he started to get a little antsy. I asked him if there were anything special that he would like to eat. He may have been only two, but even a two-year-old knows when he is getting a forbidden snacking opportunity from an unsuspecting adult. He jumped at the chance to pick out a treat. He just had to have some Hostess cupcakes. No sooner had he done that than I realized I was going to have a chocolate-covered Jake very soon, but as it turned out, he didn't want to eat them as much as he just wanted to have them. He absolutely treasured them and hugged the package tight during his nap. When he woke up he had completely flattened his cupcakes, but he still treasured them the way a gourmand hoards his caviar.

We decided that we loved having a child around the house.

When I finally got pregnant with Andy, I continued to skate. The doctor said it was okay for me because I was used to the routine and wasn't putting any new stresses on my body. I didn't know how long I would be able to continue, because I had never been through this before, and I didn't notice any difficulty until the fifth month, when I started to look not quite so elegant on the ice. Throwing more chiffon into my costumes pretty well distracted attention from my expanding middle up until the end of the second trimester. But there comes a point in every pregnancy that posture and sucking in your stomach doesn't hide things, no matter how hard you try.

My sister Maxine was traveling with me, helping me out, and being a buddy on the road. During the shows she would sit in the audience. One day she overheard a couple of ladies commenting during my performance. "Gee, Peggy looks like she has put on some weight, doesn't she?"

That was it. Time to hang up the skates for the first time since I was a little girl.

The pregnancy went well, and labor and delivery were as fine as they ever are. We arrived home with Andy. *"Okay,"* I thought, *"now what do I do?"* That was when good old-fashioned instinct kicked in, instinct and love. A friend once said that having a child opens a new room in your heart, one that you never knew was there. Andy certainly did that for Greg and me, and then, eleven years later, Todd came along and opened a whole other room. Todd got the benefit of what we had learned with Andy. The main thing I learned was that I hadn't learned all that much and that I needed to respond to my second child almost as if he were my first. Like every marriage and every friendship, I think every parent-child relationship is its own thing where both sides learn as they go.

I learned and I kept on working. Except for a six month layoff to deliver Andy, I stayed on the go—skating, performing, being in public. I took Andy to everything, and Andy enjoyed himself to the hilt. He treated every place as his playground, even if it was the home of the President.

I have been to the White House to meet five presidents, and each time was a thrill, but nothing was as much fun as the time that Greg and Andy, who was three at the time, went with me to the White House to meet Jimmy and Roslyn Carter for a Christmas at the White House event.

There was a very family feel to the Carter White House.

Both the president and first lady were very easy to be around. The Carters had a Christmas tree and a gingerbread house that Andy loved, which delighted the president and first lady. In the afternoon, during rehearsals, the president pulled a sled around on the lawn, and Andy was deliriously happy at the novelty of a sleigh ride. I could have been visiting my uncle or an old friend of the family—it was that casual.

They had made a rink on the lawn where I was to perform. I remember being in a backstage tent feeling very chilly in my skimpy skating outfit.

I looked out from behind the curtain and saw Greg sitting in the front row, right next to President Carter, who apparently wanted Andy to sit on his lap. Like the true California kid that he was and is, Andy was much more interested in snow—which he had never seen—than he was in another middle-aged man, even if this one lived in the White House. Greg was very frustrated. "The president is asking you to sit on his lap," he reasoned.

"No," Andy said, "I don't want to. I just want to play in the snow."

So Andy played in the snow. He didn't even care about seeing me do my numbers. No big deal, he must have thought, I see Mom all the time. Even though I knew how Greg probably wanted to give Andy some forceful encouragement, neither he nor I are the kick-in-the-pants type. I got enough spankings in my childhood to know that was one thing I would not do to my kids. Scolding them—or anyone—in public is a bad thing.

Of course, there are times when we all need a talking to, but one of the lessons that makes for peace in a family, or on the job, is learning to hold your tongue until you are no longer in public. Scolding a child in front of other people is certainly something that I would never want people to see me do. People never look their best when they are angry, and the object of their anger feels needlessly ashamed.

I suppose this goes back to my childhood. I know my parents did not hide their feelings about us kids no matter where we were, but I just sort of accepted it. However, I remember getting upset when Carlo Fassi would yell instructions at me in front of the rest of the skaters. Carlo had that Italian thing about letting you know exactly how he felt whenever he felt it. He would get excited and yell things at you in the middle of your routine. One day he did that to me, and I decided I had to confront him.

"Carlo," I said respectfully, "all you accomplish by doing that to me in public is to distract me. On the day of the competition you are not going to be able to do that. I'm going to have to think things through by myself. Tell me whatever you want to tell me before I go out on the ice or after I am done, but please don't correct me during my routine, it distracts me."

Carlo must have been surprised to hear me speaking up so directly, because up until that moment I pretty much did everything that every coach ever told me to do. From that day forward, Carlo knew how I wanted to be handled, and that is how he handled me. All I needed was the courage to be upfront enough to tell him, which is something we all need to remember: People don't necessarily know how you want to be treated unless you tell them.

With Todd and Andy, I remembered that lesson. Of course I will get mad, but it goes against my grain to say anything that would ever embarrass them in public or—worse—in front of their friends. I will get them alone in the hall or in the bathroom and I will look them in the eye, making sure I have their attention. That's very important, because you can be going on at your misbehaved child and he can be totally tuning you out. When you have eye contact, your words sink in that much better. I will, as the saying goes, get right in his face and say what I have to say. Being that close and that direct means you can speak in a normal tone and the message gets across. That's the way it goes in theory anyway. Sometimes we all lose it, myself included, and sometimes, no matter how mad I get, I look in my sons' eyes and I can't stay angry. This happens a lot more with Todd than it did with Andy. I think we all tend to be a little less lenient with our firstborn. I melt pretty easily with Todd, even when he is being thoroughly naughty.

It all depends on the child and the parent. My dad could discipline me in the oddest yet most effective ways. Once in my early teens I decided smoking might be cool—everybody in the movies smoked, my dad smoked a lot, and my mom smoked for a while as well. I didn't have much trouble finding a cigarette around the house, so I went out to the garage with one of my dad's Camels and lit up. I thought I looked grown-up and cool. Right about then my father walked in, and I expected him to lower the boom, but he didn't.

"Hmm, you're smoking?" he said calmly. "Great. I feel like smoking too. Why don't we smoke together?"

Dad didn't yell or anything. In fact he was pretty friendly: He suggested that we sit there, and smoke the whole pack. I don't have to tell you that I was sick to my stomach—totally green. My dad's message came through loud and clear, and I've never smoked since.

I wish I had it in me to be that forceful when Andy decided to take up smoking, but I am not that kind of parent. I like to let my children come to their own decisions even when I disagree. As a child, Andy was very much anti smoking and he knew the hazards of tobacco. No one in Greg's family smoked, and there was no question where Greg and I stood on smoking. Beyond that, Andy knew that smoking definitely contributed to my dad's three heart attacks. But even though he had that knowledge, you can never overestimate peer pressure: Andy's friends smoked so Andy smoked. He never smoked at home, but I could tell from the smell in his car and by the way his clothes smelled. We were not happy, but at least he never smoked around Todd. That would have meant big trouble.

Greg and I let him know we disapproved, but we didn't forbid him, which wouldn't have done much good. Kids are going to make their own mistakes no matter what you do. Finally we just stopped nagging and bided our time. Then, the Christmas before last, he stopped. That was his Christmas present to us and Jamaica, then girlfriend, now wife. Jamaica had also been on his case about smoking. It's good to see your kid begin to make some responsible grown-up decisions.

Andy had such a transforming effect on our life—for the better—that we wanted to have another child pretty soon after. Easier said than done. First, I had my usual difficulty getting pregnant, and then when I did, the problems had only just begun.

In 1986 I became pregnant and went in for my sonogram, which they recommend if the mother is older than her early thirties. Things didn't look right. Somehow the embryo wasn't growing the way it should have. The doctors suspected it was not fully attached to the umbilical cord, so that very afternoon I went for a D&C.

I was really down, but somehow I kept my emotions in check, telling myself it just wasn't meant to be. Luckily, I was in the middle of a production and had to do some filming at Lake Arrowhead. Once again work and skating took my mind off of problems. I had a job to do, and I thought as long as my body could physically do it—and there was no problem with that, even with the surgery—I would just have to ride herd on the emotional part and carry on with life.

But Greg and I weren't giving up. We were determined to expand our little family in our hilltop home.

Five or six months later, I was pregnant again, just before I was due to leave for Paris to cover an event for ABC. A day or two before I was to leave I began to spot. Not wanting to take any chances, I went to my OB/GYN.

"What's going on?" I asked.

Just as directly, he answered, "You're miscarrying."

Once again, the pregnancy was over without my having much of a chance to think about it. It just happened, and then I had to get on a plane. No problem, according to the doctor, "It will be like a heavy period."

Easy for the doctor to say. Thirteen hours in a plane with a heavy period is doable, but definitely no fun. Losing a second baby midflight was awful. I was really down and feeling sorry for myself, and I needed some shoulders to cry on. Greg was great on the phone, but it was still just the phone. Thankfully my ABC buddies were also there for me, but I was beginning to reach my limit of disappointment: As much as we wanted another child, Greg and I had decided we'd make one more try and then call it quits if it didn't work out.

It worked out. I set a Peggy Fleming personal-best record for getting pregnant in a hurry. Counting backward and figuring out what happened and when, it seems that my cycle was completely out of whack. Much to my surprise, we conceived Todd during a ski trip to Park City, barely six weeks after my return from Paris. I didn't realize that I was expecting until just before the Calgary Olympics in 1988. We were having a birthday party for Andy at home and I felt funny. Actually, I wasn't feeling funny—I was feeling pregnant. It didn't make sense. I had just had a miscarriage, and I didn't think you could get pregnant that quickly again. Todd is living proof that you can.

Right after the birthday party, I ran over to the drugstore and picked up a home pregnancy test. I returned home, went to the bathroom and once again I was pregnant and getting ready to go on the road!

The first thought I had was *"Oh my God, pregnant at the Olympics!"* I was worried about the long hours and the effect it would have on me, but the doctor said there was no reason not to go as long as I remembered to take care of myself and not push too hard. I was bound and determined to do whatever I had to do to keep from miscarrying. At age forty I just didn't want to think about getting older and still trying to get pregnant. This was the last try for Greg and me.

I didn't want to let anyone know about this pregnancy. If something had gone wrong, I could not face telling everyone again, Andy especially. He had gotten his hopes up twice now, and I didn't want to dash them again. As for my ABC family, they did not need to be involved in my personal life again. So I did my work and kept my mouth shut. There was plenty to do at the Olympics that year, the year of Katarina Witt and Brian Boitano.

I remember Dorothy Hamill being pregnant then as well.

She was at exactly the same stage that I was, and our children ended up being born one day apart. She was flushed with pride and hope and talked about it with everybody. I was happy too and dying to share my news, but I kept my secret all through the Olympics.

One of my fondest memories of this pregnancy is when we told Andy that Todd was on the way. We made a video that I never tire of watching—and my friends say I never tire of showing. It was a lot about our family, and about our love of games and fun and each other. In another life, Greg might have been a producer. He loves getting an idea, thinking through all the little details, and executing it. Rather than simply telling Andy, "Mom's pregnant again," we decided to make an event out of it, kind of a treasure hunt. Greg spent the better part of a morning hiding clues around the house.

When Andy put all the clues together the message spelled out: Y-O-U-R B-A-B-Y B-R-O-T-H-E-R A-R-R-I-V-E-S I-N S-E-P-T-E-M-B-E-R.

You should have seen the look on his face. He just lit up and then he started to cry. Children let their emotions come through in ways that adults find difficult. Not that day, however—all three of us had lots of tears of happiness.

Like most parents, I expected child number two to be a rerun of child number one. I was also worried that, with all the love I was lavishing on Andy, how would I have any left over for this new person?

Of course I was wrong on both counts. Todd was Todd, which meant he definitely wasn't—and isn't—Andy. And as for finding room for more love in my heart—I guess moms are made with infinite room.

Where Andy was always an athlete, that's not the major

thing in Todd's life, although we encourage him to get involved, and this year he has seemed to enjoy Little League. I am not my mom, and I am not bound and determined to make any child of mine into a champion athlete, but I think athletics are so important in many ways for every child. So many parents ask me about starting their children off in sports—it's probably the question I am asked the most. I cannot tell you how to make your child an Olympic champion, nor do I think that is particularly important. What is important is getting them good instruction in the very beginning so that they develop good basics as a matter of habit. This is the key thing, because bad habits are easy to fall into and so hard to break. Learning proper technique means, among other things, that your child is less likely to get hurt as a result of a mistake. Because they are learning the sport the right way, there is every likelihood that they will advance faster, which only makes it more fun for the child. Rather than struggling, she or he is going to make progress, and as long as there is progress, the child will be less likely to give up.

Whatever the sport is, it's important to encourage kids to be athletic. Before I began skating I had played baseball, I had been been a committed monkey bar climber, and I pretty much joined in any game I could. By the time I was introduced to skating when I was nine years old, I was coordinated enough to advance more quickly than a girl who hadn't been so involved with sports. In short, I could learn easily. When I went to skating practice I was able to master the challenge of doing what the coach asked, which made learnng more fun. It kept being fun, so I stayed with it because it was easy. That is the key to getting hooked on something—if they can do it easily children will stay with it—whether it is sport or art. Their natural ability will take them the rest of the way.

Andy's friends were all into sports—watching them and playing them. Not Todd's crowd, and we all know the importance of friends in determining what a child will want to do. So Greg and I spend time with Todd on whatever sports he does decide to play.

Andy showed great promise in tennis, but he gave it up as he became a teenager. We didn't push him because we realized that Andy, at that point, wasn't going to be a bear-down kind of athlete. He was always an easygoing kid. He never would sweat or fret over things. In this he is a lot like my dad, very happy-go-lucky. There are times when Greg and I have wished that Andy would bear down and focus more, but on the other hand, not getting worked up over things has stood him in good stead.

For instance, there was the time that Andy was president of the ski club in high school. He had organized a trip for the whole group to fly up to Vancouver. When they got to the airport the plane was overbooked. Two people would have to give up their seats. Andy and his best friend, Sean, volunteered and ending up camping out overnight at the airport. When Andy told me this, my reaction was, "Oh, Andy, that must have been horrible for you."

"No way, Mom," he answered. "We met a lot of people, we had fun checking things out at the airport. We had fun!" Only Andy could turn a "bummer" like that into a fun adventure.

Todd is different. He is always cheerful like his brother, but not quite as happy-go-lucky. Part of it has to do with his being the second-born. He also gets cut a lot of slack that his brother didn't enjoy. I learned with Andy that a lot of the anxiety that parents experience comes from entering into a strange new world. Being the parent of an eight-year-old doesn't necessarily prepare you for the experience of being the parent of a ten-year-old. You just have to go through it and learn as you go. With Todd, I had already been on that voyage into the unknown, so I learned not to be so anxious with every little thing.

Todd is much more in his own little world. He can draw beautifully, much better than Greg or Andy or me. He can amuse himself, on the computer, or out in his tree fort. Even when he is all alone, he is not alone: I hear him out there talking to his imaginary cohorts in whatever tree fort battle Todd is leading.

Of course, just when you think you have them pegged, they do something that makes you realize inside these little people there lurks a crafty person who has learned some grown-up wiles . . . often from their parents and often without their parents' knowledge. I still think of Todd as being in that Never Never Land of young kids, but somehow he's absorbed production smarts from being around my business—television.

"I want to be an ABC cameraman," he announced.

"That's great, " I said encouragingly, "but you'll need a little experience before ABC will hire you."

"No problem, Mom, I'm going to make a video of the puppet show at art class."

So I lent him my videocamera, and Todd was the director and producer of a puppet show about the circus. When Greg and I went to the show, there was Todd doing just what he had seen me do when I have an on-camera.

"Okay everybody," he said, pulling himself up to his fifty-two inches "In 5–4–3–2–1. . . . Action!"

I struggled not to burst out laughing.

Next, Todd wanted to be the one at the center of attention, just like Mom. Recently he decided to run for student council.

"I've never won anything, Mom. I really want to do this."

Todd liked the idea of running for office, until he realized he would also have to write the speech. It was tough for him so I offered to help. He accepted my offer—sort of. He wanted me to do the actual physical writing, but he didn't want me telling him what to say.

"I'll talk. You write," Todd said. He had definitely reached the I-can-do-it-myself stage. So he talked and I wrote *exactly* as he said it.

"Now you have to practice," I told him. This was necessary advice, because he has a tendency to drop his head and his voice. "Remember how when I have to do something on ABC, I go around the house and pronounce my words very clearly. I underline the words that I really want to get across the most so that I have a reminder about what is important when I am reading."

Todd listened intently and practiced. The best part of the whole event, and the one that showed how much he had picked up from television, was this little sticker he made. It was red, white, and blue and it read "Vote for Todd." I told him to pin it to his shirt when he read. I also told him that maybe when he was done with the speech he might want to take out a little American flag and wave it—a kind of a cute attention-getter that would make people remember him.

He thought that was a silly idea and didn't even try to humor me. "No, Mom, I'm not going to do that," he pronounced with finality. But I could see I had planted something in his directorial mind. He went to school, gave the speech, and didn't make a mistake. On the back of the last page of the speech—visible for everyone to see—he had pasted his sticker: "I am Todd Jenkins. Vote for Me." He was thinking how things look from the camera (or audience point of view). He won the election.

I have to get used to the fact that even my little Todd is starting to become an independent person. He was always asking about the places I traveled to when I was working. He never went on the road with me like his big brother had. I was eleven years older than I had been with Andy and less up to the rigors of traveling, working, and having a child with me. So when I went out on the road, more often to broadcast than to perform, I kissed my family good-bye and hit the road for a week or two; never more than that. I wouldn't take the job if it required a longer stay away from home.

Still, Todd was very curious about what it was like to be on the road with Mom.

"Todd," I told him one day, "if you have something of yours that you want me to take with you, that would be terrific. That way, whenever you ask me what a certain place is like, I can tell you. Then when I come home and give you back your special thing, that part of you will have been everywhere I have been."

And so Todd's shoe went on tour with me. One night when I called home from Sofia, Bulgaria, Todd said he had an important question for me. "Mom, what does the phone look like? Is it different from one of our phones at home?"

"Honey, I'm going to put your shoe next to that phone and take a picture of it."

"That's great, Mom. How about the people on the street? What do they look like?"

So I put Todd's shoe on a busy street and snapped a picture: Todd's shoe with a crowd of Bulgarians.

Todd got the biggest kick out of it. To see something as familiar as a shoe in front of the Eiffel Tower or on a frozen Russian canal made him feel like a part of him was there.

The affair of Todd's shoe came to a climax when we were in Canada covering the World championships in Edmonton. It was another one of those slow days on the set, and I asked Jim McKay—ABC's voice of the Olympics—to interview Todd's shoe. Jim was game.

In his most Olympic voice, Jim talked into the microphone.

"Ladies and Gentlemen, we have brought you many unforgettable moments over the years but truly nothing quite like this one. To my knowledge this is the first time that any commentator has had the opportunity to interview the shoe of Todd Jenkins, son of Olympic champion Peggy Fleming. How does it feel to be here today?"

In a stunning close-up, Todd's shoe didn't answer.

Hey, we had time to kill in Edmonton. Todd enjoyed knowing that his was the first (and no doubt the last) shoe to be interviewed by ABC Sports.

Being away from my family is tough. I hate to miss any part of the boys's childhood, and I really can't stand not being there when my boys need their mom. But you do what you have to, and I have to be on the road more than I would like, even though I love what I do.

Sometimes, though, things happen in your children's lives not according to your schedule. Actually they don't happen according to *any* schedule.

When Todd was nearly three, I was at an appearance in Chicago and Greg was at a rowing camp, the Craftsbury

Sculling School in Vermont. Our neighbor, Amy Gillum, was baby-sitting the boys for a few days, and one evening after dinner, she took them down to the yogurt store in town.

Todd was seated at a low chair, but he was so small that his legs didn't reach the ground. When he went to get out of the chair he had to lean on the marble-topped table to push his chair back. The table was not balanced too well, and when Todd pushed down on it, it tipped over. Todd fell to the floor and the tabletop came down right on his right hand, breaking his middle finger and, worse, almost completely severing his index finger.

Todd was in terrible pain, and there wasn't an adult around —just our young neighbor Amy, the high-school kid behind the counter, and Andy. Todd was beside himself, but Andy had the presence of mind to wrap up his finger and to hold it secure and get 911 called. He had the even greater presence of mind to keep Todd distracted with candy so that he never saw his finger: he kept it wrapped until they got Todd into microsurgery, where they saved the finger.

Meanwhile, first Amy and then the doctor called me and I was frantic: There was no way to get back to Los Gatos until the following morning. With Greg temporarily unreachable for a number of hours in the backwoods of Vermont, I have never felt so helpless in my life. There was my poor little baby having to go through this ordeal, and neither of his parents was there.

As soon as I reached his room the next day, I saw my little one all groggy on painkillers. He looked at me and burst into tears, and I followed suit. I stayed with him at the hospital for four days and nights. It was a truly terrible time and, even as I write this, I still marvel that Andy had the presence of mind to handle Todd the way he did. Otherwise Todd would surely have lost his finger. They were always close as brothers, but I noticed a deeper attachment since that ordeal.

The lesson that came home to me after Todd's experience at the yogurt store is that nobody—not the most loving mom, the most concerned dad—can be there all the time. Things are going to happen. Even after you weather the storms of childhood, the surprises still come. The most recent one—the one that led to the birth of my adorable grandson—shook the whole family up.

When Andy was at the University of Denver, he became friendly with a student from a little town in New Hampshire, Jamaica Beaudin, a pretty outdoorsy young lady who shares Andy's interests in sports. They had a lot in common. They took a lot of the same classes together and they both loved snowboarding in the Colorado mountains whenever they had the chance. They also lived in the same dorm.

In their minds they were just "best friends," but when two attractive young people spend a lot of time together, it often surprises nobody—except the couple involved—when they have become more than friends. Andy and Jamaica realized this at the end of her freshman year when Jamaica moved to Santa Monica. Very shortly, Andy discovered that he missed Jamaica terribly. He sent her love letters and, the modern equivalent, videos. When he sent her a ring engraved with the words *I love you,* Jamaica knew that my happy-go-lucky son was serious about her. The pull of young love was too strong, and Jamaica moved back to Colorado.

Love and growing up, however, are two different things. Andy spent his sophomore year in a bachelor pad with his buddies—getting an education but not missing too many opportunities to party. Jamaica was ready for a serious commitment: Andy wasn't sure, even though he was crazy about Jamaica.

Jamaica buried herself in work as a student, waitress, and part-time nanny. Andy continued with his studies and his buddies, but both of them felt something was missing. The best friends needed each other more deeply than they had known at the beginning of the school year. By the time Andy let us know that he was going to share the driving with Jamaica on a summer trip back to New Hampshire, the young couple had an extra passenger. Jamaica was pregnant.

Andy found out just before the road trip. Greg and I found out one afternoon shortly thereafter. I had just returned from a four-mile run in the hills with my girlfriends. Waiting for me was one of those surprises that always blindside a parent. They often start with a phone call.

"Mom, I need to talk to you," Andy said. Usually this kind of conversation is a prelude to needing new tires for his truck, or some help with other expenses.

"I'm late for an appointment, Andy," I said, "can it wait?"

"Actually, I really do need to talk with you. It's kind of important."

The appointment could wait, I decided. "What is it, Andy, are you in trouble?"

"Jamaica's pregnant," he answered.

My first reaction was one of frustration, even anger. "How could they let this happen?" I asked myself. Inside, though, underneath my motherly pique, there was another motherly reaction, one that knew that these things happen all the time. It's called being human—or in the case of Andy and Jamaica: young, human, and in love. I had no problem with them as a couple. I just wished they had taken their time getting started in life before having a child.

But children very rarely follow the imaginary, well-intentioned scripts that their parents write for them. The reality of the situation was that my grandchild was on the way. The news was not greeted with enthusiasm by Greg. His son had really made a mistake, the kind that could not be fixed with money or a self-help book. But no matter what we thought, we weren't in charge of Andy's life anymore.

Every parent knows that there comes a day when the child takes control of his or her own life. Actually, it is more accurate to say there comes a time when power begins to be handed over gradually. In the case of my mother, I didn't feel fully at the controls until I was in my mid-thirties, but Andy was on a much more accelerated course.

Abortion wasn't an option. Neither was adoption. Jamaica was determined to raise her child. It was unplanned, but this baby was going ahead. Greg and I were concerned that Andy was making a serious change in his life without the opportunity to comprehend how big a change and how big a responsibility it would be. I could see the pressure taking its toll on him.

It took Andy a while to get his thoughts clear. That June he came home to be with us and to think about reality with a capital *R*. He needed to ask himself what it meant to be a father, to understand the responsibilities of fatherhood, and while he did that, to assess his relationship with Jamaica. They were joined in parenthood, but did that mean that it would be best if they were joined for life? It came down to that one word that sends many young men—and a lot of older ones too—heading for the exit: *commitment*. Could Andy make a lifetime commitment?

It was a tough time for Andy. It was a tough time and a soul-searching time—for our whole family. We all had to dig deep and figure out who we were as a family, the Jenkins family. How could we truly make this work?

We went to a family counselor—the three of us—and talked a lot. The talking and the time helped clear things up in Andy's mind: If Jamaica was going to have the baby, then Andy felt he could not sit by without helping her. He felt that he had to continue in the right way. Ultimately he decided that he couldn't live with the baby growing up without him around, and he decided to be with Jamaica and the baby.

This wasn't the way I imagined Andy entering his twenty-second year, but I began to look at the bright side: My son was making decisions that showed he had a deep sense of personal responsibility. Once he made the decision to see things through with Jamaica—in other words, once he had sorted out his confused feelings—I was fine with it. It surprised me how fine I was. Maybe a mother knows inside when something is good for her child, even when things don't go according to plan.

Andy was going back East, to New Hampshire, where Jamaica would have the baby. He packed up his truck, just like he and I had done when he first went to college. He gave Todd a big hug, and all of us were a little weepy. My first baby was really off on his own now! Although Greg and I are always there for him, we felt that becoming a parent doesn't mean your parents continue to support you like it's just another college course. We felt that if you're going to take a big step, one of the other big steps that comes along with it is working hard to make sacrifices as you go. Inside, of course, I knew that while we had to say that, we would end up helping the newest Jenkins family.

John Curry and I rehearsing in my backyard in Atherton in 1981. We used the sliding-glass doors as mirrors. (Collection of the author)

Robin Cousins and I freezing in Rockefeller Center in 1982. We were filming the "Radio City Music Hall Christmas Special" and we shot from midnight until six A.M. (Collection of the author)

Toller Cranston, me and Robin Cousins at "Ice" at Radio City Music Hall. (Photo by Christie Jenkins/Los Angeles)

Dorothy Hamill and I during the "100th Anniversary of the Statue of Liberty" special in 1986. (Collection of the author)

In Boston, 1993, at the first Skates of Gold event. From left: Anett Potzsch, me, JoJo Starbuck, Katarina Witt and Kristi Yamaguchi. (Courtesy of Jean Hall)

Al Joyner, me and Florence Griffith Joyner in 1997. (Courtesy of Jean Hall)

Michelle Kwan, me and Dorothy Hamill in 1997. (Courtesy of Jean Hall)

Lu Chen, after her second-place finish at the 1996 World Championships in Edmonton, Alberta. (Courtesy of Jean Hall)

Brian Boitano gives me a squeeze at the 1998 U.S. Nationals in Philadelphia. (Photo by Beverly Peyton)

Michelle Kwan, me and Carlo Fassi at Lake Arrowhead. (Courtesy of Jean Hall)

Dorothy Hamill, Robin Cousins and me at Carlo Fassi's tribute in August 1997. (Courtesy of Leah Adams)

During the finale of the "Ave Maria" that I skated at the tribute for Carlo. (Copyright Cindy Lang)

Leslie Visser, Brian Boitano, me and Terry Gannon at the 1998 U.S. Nationals in Philadelphia. (Courtesy of Jean Hall)

Dick Button and I outside a café in Vienna (where they are famous for their chocolate cake) during the 1967 World Championships. (Photograph by Ulli Skoruppa, courtesy of BUNTE)

At the 1988 Olympics in Calgary with Dick. I'm three months' pregnant with Todd. (Collection of the author)

Three "glamour shots" from a 1994 photo shoot. (Courtesy of Harry Langdon)

Greg and me on our twenty-fifth wedding anniversary, June 13, 1995.
(Collection of the author)

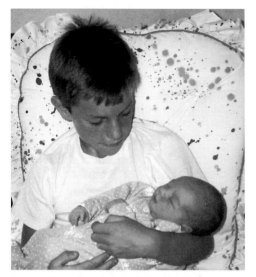

September 21, 1988. Andy holding his three-day-old brother, Todd. (Collection of the author)

Andy and Todd sledding in Squaw Valley in 1991. (Collection of the author)

The boys making chocolate chip cookies in our kitchen. (Collection of the author)

Like father, like son: Todd and Greg in 1993. (Collection of the author)

The two Todds: my Todd and Todd Eldridge during the 1995 *Nutcracker* tour. (Collection of the author)

Jim McKay gamely interviewing Todd's shoe at the 1996 World Championships in Edmonton, Alberta. (Courtesy of Jean Hall)

With my friends Pam Wethington, Jean Hall and Karol MacDonald in the San Juan Islands in 1997. (Courtesy of Jean Hall)

My men and I going out for dinner to celebrate my fiftieth birthday. (Collection of the author)

The three boys all dressed up at the Cancer Award Dinner in Denver, Colorado, in May 1998. (Collection of the author)

My friend Martha Neumann and me (I'm not the one in the middle!) at the Rancho La Puerta Health Spa in Mexico, right after the cancer surgery in 1998. (Courtesy of Martha Neumann)

Wendy Reagan, my cheerful "radiation friend," in 1998. (Collection of the author)

The ABC crew being supportive after my cancer diagnosis kept me away from the World Championships in 1998. (Courtesy of Tami Mickle)

Vera Wang fitting me for a costume in 1998. (Courtesy of Vera Wang)

Andy, Jamaica, and Miles hiking in Craftsbury, Vermont, in July 1999. (Collection of the author)

The whole family together in Vermont in July 1999. (Collection of the author)

Andy and Jamaica rented a small condo on Lake Horace in Weare, New Hampshire. By September, they had both transferred into new schools and were working full-time jobs. They took classes at night and Andy worked days as a land surveyor while Jamaica was a teacher's aide in a middle school. Andy was settling in and settling down. He seemed to grow up more day by day, even mentioning the "E Word": *engagement.*

Meanwhile the West Coast Jenkins were starting to feel good about becoming grandma and grandpa. After raising two boys and dealing with wall-too-wall sweat socks, messy rooms, toy trucks, and other guy stuff, I had often dreamed about the possibility of having a granddaughter. We would do all those special girl things—shopping, trying on clothes, and making cookies, little things that add up to so much of the joy in life.

But the most satisfying part of the Long Program of life isn't necessarily completing the most difficult jumps. It's having all the little moves go well.

D-Day—Jamaica's due date—was February sixth. I started a countdown on the chalk board in my kitchen. When D-Day came and went, I started keeping track of the days that the baby was overdue. I was a nervous wreck, and I leaped at every phone call. My friends ratcheted up the anticipation and the anxiety by calling regularly to get the news, as if I wouldn't have called all of them the minute it happened.

On February eighteenth, Andy called. They were going to induce labor the next day. Greg and I looked at each other. That next day was the sixth anniversary of the death of Greg's mother. Andy had surprised and gratified us both when he delivered a beautiful eulogy at Grandma Betty's memorial service.

On that sad day, Andy had taken a first big step toward

growing up. Now six years years later, on a much happier day, he was taking another step on the road to becoming a man. It seemed right, somehow, that Grandma Betty would be in the picture. And he called repeatedly as the day moved along, giving us updates on the mother-to-be's progress, which was slow. It was even possible that inducing wouldn't work and they would have to go home and wait a while longer to see if the baby came all on its own.

We sat down that night to a special dinner: I made a marinated pork tenderloin that I learned during my days as spokesperson for the National Pork Producers Council—it was and remains a family favorite. We even drank a nice bottle of French wine to celebrate and relax a little, but truthfully, it was hard to relax. Now that there was a possibility that the baby would be born on a day of special family significance, Greg and I were rooting for our grandchild to be born before the day ended.

The stars were in our favor. With fifteen minutes left, Miles Andrew Jenkins gave his first cry. I was a grandmother. For just the teeniest split second I thought, "Guess I'll have to return all those little girl things I bought"—and then Greg and I smiled and hugged one another. I don't think I ever remember being happier. When I won my gold medal, I had a crowd around, giving me a case of nerves. When my own children were born, I was so worn out from the labor that it was hard to feel anything else except relief that it was over. But being told you are a grandparent doesn't require any crowd-pleasing or physical exertion. The only thing you have to do is be happy, and we were.

Now I just had to see that baby. A week later I was scheduled to go to Russia to cover an event for ABC Sports, so I arranged to stop over in New Hampshire and see Miles for myself. I took enough planes and made enough connections on that trip to go around the world. Los Gatos, California, and Weare, New Hampshire, are not exactly major airline hubs. On the other end of the trip, there wasn't a direct connection from New Hampshire to St. Petersburg, so I knew I was in for some heavy road dues.

Still, I was just about jumping out of my skin with anticipation at seeing my eight-pound grandson. I pictured the whole family waiting for me with smiles and waves as I came off the plane, but when I came out of the arrival gate, there was no one there. I thought maybe the wintry roads had slowed them, or maybe they weren't able to make it at all.

"Oh well, it will be what it will be," I thought as I took the escalator to baggage-claim. There, at the bottom of the escalator were Andy and Jamaica . . . and *Miles!* Jamaica handed the baby to me, and I hugged and cooed and gave off enough squeals of delight to attract everyone's attention in the airport. All these strangers saw me beaming at this little child and came up to congratulate our family.

I held Miles the whole time we were in baggage and all the way out to the car before we put him in his little baby seat. I spent the next few days around Miles as much as I could before I had to take the plane over to St. Petersburg.

I did my job, even enjoyed some marvelous skating, but couldn't wait to be back home with my grandson again. Greg arranged to take some time off, and Todd also had a very fortuitous school vacation, so we rented a beautiful cabin on a lake near to Andy's family.

It was ideal: a big fireplace, and lots of snow outside.

Andy, who was working as a snowboard instructor, gave lessons to Todd and Greg. I tried it, even liked it, but all I really wanted to do was sit in front of the fire and cuddle with Miles, which is exactly what I did. There are few moments in life that are perfect—when you are healthy and happy and so is your family and you feel closeness and warmth and the special joy of contentment. That time in New Hampshire was one of them.

As I write these words, spring has come and gone in New Hampshire and Andy has been working with Jamaica's father building houses and attending school. Having a baby has been good for Andy in so many ways. Having a wife—they'll be married by the time this book comes out!—has been good too. Jamaica is a perfect match for Andy: athletic and lots of fun, but with a maturity that has helped the relationship.

Being a grandmother so soon was never part of my Long Program any more than being a dad at age twenty-two was part of Andy's, but we're happy and it's working out for all of us.

I'm looking out the window at the brush-covered hills that begin across from our front gate and go as far as the eye can see. After our house, there is nothing but brush and animals and rock. It's been that way forever, or at least as long as anyone around here can remember.

Last week we took a step to change that. Greg and I had some of the land cleared, the brush cut away and buried, and our two acres planted with grapes vines. We're going to have a vineyard: the Jenkins Vineyard. We're going to make a crisp California Chardonnay—elegant, with lots of power, just like good skating.

Andy, Jamaica, and Miles came for their first visit just after we put in the young vines. Jamaica was wearing the engagement ring that Andy had given her, a simple solitaire setting, just like the ring Greg had given me. I was so touched—touched, because my little boy is getting married and touched because he gave his future wife the same kind of ring that his mom still wears.

We walked in the vineyard. Those hills were Andy and Todd's playground. Their skateboard half-pipe (that's what real skateboarders practice on) had been there and so was the brush where they had fought all those imaginary battles that young boys fight.

I took a picture of Andy's new family with Uncle Todd standing alongside, all holding farm implements:—well, all except Miles. I wanted to have this picture of our family's future in their future vineyard.

Lots of new growth there, it made my motherly and grandmotherly heart swell.

"Have you ever driven your Range Rover around the vineyard, Mom?" Andy asked.

I told him I hadn't. I didn't want to get my car all banged up and covered with dust from the hills. Later, when we went inside and I was puttering around the house, Andy asked if he could borrow the car "to do errands."

I said sure, and went back to what I was doing. A while later, I looked out the window and there was Andy behind the wheel of my Range Rover, giving a pretty good impression of what a four-wheel-drive commercial would look like if they ever shot one in our hills.

"Awesome, Mom," he said as he pulled my dust-covered Rover into the garage.

I thought to myself, "It must be a boy thing," but then I remembered that there was a time when the tomboy inside of that little ice skater from Morgan Hill would have wanted to take that drive for herself.

But grandmas don't do things like that, I told myself.

Well, at least not when the kids are around.

My Wake-Up Call

ome people run from stress, but I've always felt that you have to take a stand and confront it. It doesn't matter what the stress is—you have to look it in the eye and back it down, otherwise it will beat you every time, whether it is the risk of failure, a disease attacking you from within, or a stranger lurking in the woods. I have faced them all. I believe I am stronger than they are and so are you.

First, the stranger in the woods: One July when I had some free time and a pile of frequent flier mileage, Jean and I and a group of friends took a trip to the Galápagos Islands, which are about as far as you can get from everywhere. The wildlife, the scenery—it was a step back in time. One day our group had brunch on an isolated beach and, rather than return to the main village by boat, Jean and I decided to walk the four or five miles by ourselves.

We dropped our backpacks in the sand and took a stroll down the beach. We must have gone around two hundred yards when I turned around to take in the beautiful view, and there was this guy running into the trees . . . with our two backpacks!

Jean and I took off after him, yelling and screaming as we went. The sight of two banshees in bikinis must have been too much for this Galápagos purse-snatcher. He dropped our bags and hightailed into the woods.

"Good thing we decided against skinny-dipping," I said to Jean. If we didn't catch him it would have been awfully embarrassing to walk into the nearest village trying to preserve our dignity with some leaves from a rubber plant.

Having rescued our bags, we began the walk back to the village, which we were told would take about an hour and a half. The path led along the shore and through a thorn-filled scrub forest. There were a few hills that the tour people said had a really pretty view.

We didn't give much thought to our brush with the pack-snatcher until we turned around, and there he was again, about a hundred yards behind us.

We stopped.

He stopped.

"Peggy," said Jean, "I think our boyfriend is after us again."

We ran as fast as we could. When we got to the top of a little rise we looked back, and there he was, running flat out. There was no question about it: He was pursuing us.

Jean said, "We are not going to outrun this guy. I think it's better to face him now, while we are fresh, than a hour from now when we are deep in the woods."

I agreed.

We knew, or at least we were pretty sure, that he didn't have a gun. If anything, he had a knife. We turned our knapsacks around so that we were wearing them in front; that way if he slashed out at us, we had a little protection. Next we needed weapons and when you are in the middle of the forest, you do like the cavemen did: You pick up something that's lying around. I grabbed a big spiky piece of cactus, and Jean grabbed a couple of softball-sized lava rocks.

We headed a little bit farther down the path, around a blind curve, and we waited. A couple of minutes later our attacker came loping around the curve, and when he saw us, he stopped dead in his tracks and tried to act nonchalant. We walked very fast straight toward him. I'm sure he thought we were nuts.

Jean knocked her stones together, and I did my best to look dangerous with my cactus war club. Neither of us speaks Spanish, but we communicated pretty well that we wanted him to keep on walking, *ahead of us.* There was no way we were going to let him sneak up on us from behind.

He said a lot of things in very fast Spanish, but the only word I picked out was *loco* which he kept muttering all the way to town. When we reached it—actually it was more like a little village—we went our way and he went his. We were glad to see the last of him.

I don't tell you this story to encourage you to pick up a stick the next time you think somebody is following you. I have always thought it is better to walk away from trouble. But sometimes trouble seeks you out and you can't walk away. It is much better to confront it immediately, before it wears you down.

Breast cancer was that kind of trouble. In 1998, the story started in January, which is usually a special month for me. At least it feels that way every four years, when the world gets ready for the Olympic Winter Games. That's when the talk really heats up about who's going to win the figure skating. The magazines always have a picture of some smiling young girl in her skating costume—this year's hopeful. I get caught up in it and can't help thinking, "That was me way back when." In 1998, during the buildup to the Olympics, I was looking forward to returning to Philadelphia to cover the National championships for ABC.

Philadelphia was where I had won my last National championship and where Michelle Kwan and Tara Lipinski were about to give us one of the greatest woman-to-woman competitions that skating had ever seen. What made it even more meaningful for me was the return of the whole Olympic skating team from 1968 for our thirtieth reunion. It was going to be a milestone for me to see Tim Wood, Cindy and Ron Kauffman, Judy Schwomeyer, and Jim Sladky once again.

I really wanted to be my best. Anyone who has ever gone to a college reunion after twenty or so years knows what I mean: You take extra time with your makeup and hair, and you want the outfit that makes you look younger and slimmer.

Getting ready for work in Philadelphia one evening, I felt tired. The pressure of the event, my work, and seeing my old colleagues was a lot for one day. I looked in the mirror. As I did, I stretched and noticed something. There, in the shadow thrown by the overhead light in the hotel bathroom, I thought I noticed a little lump on my chest. I kind of dismissed it. *Maybe it's a muscle I pulled in my workout. Being in a strange town on strange exercise equipment can do that.*

I wasn't totally convinced. Something made me keep on looking at that little lump or whatever it was. I remember thinking, "Hmmm, that's strange," as I rubbed it. It definitely did not feel like a muscle, and it definitely was a lump. I looked at the other side of my chest, and there was nothing there. It was just smooth. Although I made a note to have it looked at, I wasn't alarmed because I'd gone for my checkup recently and was given a clean bill of health.

Still, there was something there, so I did what I always do when something happens on the road: I asked Jean what she thought.

"I have a lump here," I said.

Jean said, " Gosh, It is a lump. You had better get that checked right away."

"Look, I just had a mammogram and everything was fine. It's probably nothing," I said. In reality, we were both worried but trying, in our own ways, to keep the anxiety under control. Then I told Greg what was up. He too gave the standard reassurances, but I could hear the concern in his voice as well

Michelle Kwan skated her most memorable program, and I finished my job at the Nationals. From Philadelphia we moved directly on to Milan for the European championships. During the whole time I kept looking at my lump, which was lasting a lot longer than any muscle pull. I wanted to make sure that nothing had changed since my last mammogram. I made an appointment for the day after I got back home. The lump was really grating on me. My body had always responded to care and work, but now it was doing something I didn't like. For the first time, I was afraid my body was letting me down.

I got home around seven-thirty at night on January eighteenth. Todd waited up for me and gave me a big hug. So did Greg, and it felt *so good* to have his arms around me just then. Everything was the way it was supposed to be, except for one thing, and that one thing kept me up all night.

I was the first one at the doctor's office the next morning. Todd was off from school that day so I took him along for what I thought would be a short visit. I missed him so much, and I just had to have him with me. Nothing bad could happen with Todd around, right?

Dr. Brown, my OB/GYN, examined me for a few minutes and stopped. He wasn't sure about it and said, "Yes, it is questionable. It doesn't look quite right. I am not saying it is anything to worry about, but I think for us to have peace of mind, we should get another opinion."

With Todd still in tow, I went to see Dr. Carl Bertelsen, a breast surgeon, who took one look and sent me right in for a needle biopsy. Todd wanted to stay with me to comfort me, but Dr. Bertelsen thought he'd do better if he waited outside while I had needles stuck in me. So while he stayed and read Ranger Rick in the waiting room, I went in for my biopsy.

For something so important, a needle biopsy isn't all that much of a procedure. They numb you and withdraw a little tissue. I hardly felt it. When the results came in that afternoon, the surgeon called and said it was still questionable and they wanted to take the lump out.

"Can you make it tomorrow?" he asked.

"Well, I have a performance in Boston next week and I have a hair appointment tomorrow," I answered.

Now when I write these words, I know they seem frivolous. But as I found out while going through the longest part of my own personal Long Program, the so-called "little things in life" are sometimes all that keep us from falling into despair. So there I was, with a surgeon basically telling me he was worried that I had breast cancer, and I gave the hairdresser as an excuse. Bottom line; I needed a couple of days to get my act together, but there was no putting off the inevitable.

I planned the surgery for a few days later. I arrived at the Mission Oaks Hospital in Los Gatos about five in the afternoon, one of the last patients of the day. I was sedated but conscious all through the procedure. When he reached the growth (I still shied away from calling it a tumor), Dr. Bertelsen spoke to me.

"It looks fine," he said, and showed it to me. I was expecting something gross and terrible, like in the movie *Alien,* but to my untrained and hopeful eyes it looked perfectly healthy. Of course the lab would give the final results, but for now, there was no reason not to go on with my life and my work. He stitched me up and said there was no reason I couldn't perform.

Life was going to be just fine. I left for the East at six-thirty the next morning. Even though I had just had surgery, I didn't have much pain, although the industrial-strength painkillers Dr. Bertelsen gave me might have had something to do with that. I didn't really think about it. I just felt really awful, like you do when you have a crummy flu coming on. I remember sitting there on that plane thinking, *"Oh God, I really feel downright horrible."*

I needed some rest, which was the one thing I couldn't get on my schedule. The trip to Boston coincided with a stop in Colorado Springs, where I was being inducted to the Colorado College Sports Hall of Fame. Since it would give me a chance to see Andy—who was a student at Denver University—I had been looking forward to the trip, but not under these conditions. I stole half an hour to lie down in the hotel, but then I had to go through the whole routine of showering, dressing, hair, and makeup before I went to the ceremony. I managed to get things together, but soon I began to feel sore. To make things worse, the medication was knocking me out. Since there wasn't a whole lot required of me beyond smiling and saying a few nice words at the ceremony, I got through it without anyone's being the wiser about my condition.

It was a different story back at the hotel. Greg, Todd, and Andy were there. Greg knew what was up, and Todd knew I had had surgery, although I'm not sure he really knew what the surgery was for. However, when Andy came in and gave me a big hug, he saw how I winced, and he knew something was up. I told him that the doctors thought everything would be fine, but I'm not sure he believed me.

Next, I went on to Boston to work with Robin Cousins on a show for ESPN called "A Skater's Tribute to Hollywood." If anybody else had asked me, I think I would have canceled, but it would take a lot more than a biopsy hangover to keep me from participating in something for him. Actually, I felt strong and fine and less beat up by the medicine and the surgery by the time I got to Boston. I went right to the gym for a nice long workout to see what kind of shape I was in after three days without skating. I felt better after getting some exercise. I removed some of the bandages so that they didn't bulge under my costume. Now I had to deal with the pairs number I was doing with Robin, which required him to lift me. The choreography still had to be worked out, so there would be a lot of lifting in rehearsal.

"Be careful of that area, Robin," I said. "Don't worry. It's benign," I added, even though I didn't know if that was true or not. I also let a few of the other skaters know that part of the story because it became impossible to hide.

Everyone kept the secret and the show went fine.

Meanwhile, back home, Greg got the results of the biopsy: They weren't what we were hoping to hear. I had breast cancer. They had found it early, and it was one of the less dangerous forms of cancer, and I was going to be okay. But still it was cancer. I was on the other coast, and Greg was due to fly to a medical meeting in Florida in a few hours, so he had to decide how to get the news to me. He didn't want to do it long distance, especially with a performance coming up. He felt that I would be too devastated to perform and that there was no need to upset me right then since another surgery, though indicated, would have to wait for a little while. Greg wanted to be the one to tell me the results and he wanted me to be home, where I felt most secure, when I got the news. Canceling the Florida trip wasn't an option because Greg knew me well enough to realize if he didn't go, I would put two and two together and panic. So Greg took off on schedule but set a plan in motion that would break the news to me as gently as possible.

When I arrived home, Greg's nurses, Pam and Debbie, were there. They made up some story about needing to check something about the plans for decorating Greg's offices and they wanted my opinion. I thought this was a strange time to talk about decorating the office after all my travel and the doctors and all, but if Greg needed it, then I would just do it.

After about ten minutes of small talk and color swatches, Greg called from Florida. I took the call in my office. The nurses stayed out in the kitchen. They knew what Greg was going to say and were staying around to be supportive if I needed it.

"You're going to be fine," he started out—which told me that maybe everything wasn't fine. "There is some bad news though. It was malignant and you are probably going to need more surgery, but they think they caught everything in time. Listen, honey," he said, trying to sound cheerful even though I heard his voice breaking with emotion, "the doctor will fill you in completely at your appointment." My appointment was one hour later. "Just remember I love you and you are going to be all right."

I felt like I had been hit in the stomach, and the head, and the heart. Cancer? Malignant? Those couldn't possibly be words used about me. I mean, I saw it—it didn't look that bad. The doctor said it didn't look bad either. How could I possibly have cancer?

I hung up the phone and cried. It couldn't have been too long, maybe just a couple of minutes, but even now I remember that moment. It was so painful and scary and one of the few times that I dropped my guard and let it get to me. When something big happens in life and you open yourself to your emotions—something I don't do that often—they really come on strong. Then, like after a summer storm, full of thunder and lightning, the crying stopped and I got myself together enough to come out and face Pam and Debbie.

I could tell from the way they looked at me and the questions they asked that they already knew the diagnosis. By calling just before my doctor's appointment, Greg had made sure that I got the news in the best way for me. I didn't have time to really sit down and just say, "Oh, my God, what's happening to me?" I didn't have the full story yet because I hadn't gone to the doctor's. Greg was very reassuring, but I knew that he was scared too.

Pam and Debbie stayed a few minutes to see how I was doing and then they left. I got in my car and drove to the doctor, and that's when I felt the most fear. When I got to Dr. Bertelsen's office, he began to explain things, and then I wasn't quite so scared. He drew pictures that explained the procedures I would have to go through, he showed me graphs and printouts, and he talked me through things. I began to feel better. At least I was facing the known instead of worrying about the unknown. "It is going to be all right," I kept telling myself and soon I believed it.

Dr. Bertelsen explained that I would need more surgery. He recommended a lumpectomy as well as a biopsy from the lymph nodes. Greg was due home the next day, so we scheduled the surgery for the first available opportunity.

The surgery was not complicated, but it was the most serious medical thing I had gone through since giving birth to my children. They knocked me out, took out the tissue, and when I came to, they sent me home, which was fine with me. At least I would be able to sleep in my own bed.

Waiting for the results was hell: First, there was the normal question of "Will I be all right?" The lumpectomy showed no more cancerous cells, and the lymph-node biopsies were clean as well. My chances for long-term survival went up with those pieces of news. My soul and I both breathed a big sigh of relief. Even though I continued to think positively, there was still a part of me that thought, "Hey, last time I thought it was going to be fine and then it wasn't, so *maybe* it's going to be bad news again." But I'm not the kind of person to go down the worst-case scenario path, so I hadn't let myself go there.

The other reason that the waiting period was stressful had nothing to do with my physical state—it had everything to do with Peggy Fleming, public figure. We tried to keep everything quiet until we knew for sure that I would be okay. At that point, we would release a statement through my agents at IMG, just as they had helped release the story when Scott Hamilton revealed that he had testicular cancer. I knew that my story, like Scott's, would get out, but I wanted to be the one telling the tale and not turn a private matter into a tabloid feature.

Who was I kidding? In this day and age of total news saturation, the media finds out everything. Word got out, and we began to get calls asking for confirmation. I knew there was no keeping the lid on, so Greg, Jean, and I made a phone list. We each had thirty people to call. We wanted to be the ones who told the people closest to us. Within hours of that first call asking for confirmation, the story was on CNN and then, later that day, there it was again—fittingly? ironically?—on prime time at the Olympics. It was the thirtieth anniversary of my gold medal, the night of the men's figure skating short program. The big Olympic theme came on, and the camera moved through a snow-swept Nagano landscape. It settled on Jim Nantz in his chalet-style anchor booth. After a brief update on the day's headlines he continued:

> "And we have this word regarding a legend in the sport of figure skating. Peggy Fleming underwent breast cancer surgery Tuesday in California, we have learned; and that was just one day before the thirtieth anniversary of her winning the gold medal in Grenoble. In fact, we spoke to Peggy this evening; she's resting at home in California. She told us she's tired but feeling fine and very positive about her recovery. From all of us here at CBS and I'm sure the entire nation, our thoughts and

prayers are with Peggy Fleming and her family tonight."

Was that person they were talking about really me? Headline news is where you hear that President Kennedy was shot, or that men have landed on the moon. You don't hear about me, Peggy Fleming, having breast cancer. It sounded serious, terribly grave, like I wasn't doing as well as the doctors were telling me. It sounded like the kind of announcements they make when people die. I definitely wasn't close to that—I knew that better than anybody—but when you hear it on the news, it gets bigger and more scary. I had a lump in my throat and was on the point of tears.

Shortly after the announcement, the phone rang. I was expecting that. "Hi, Peggy, this is Michelle," the caller said.

"Michelle," I thought, *"which Michelle? I know a few Michelles."* And then it dawned on me it was Michelle Kwan, calling from Nagano!

"I just heard the news," she said, "and I was real concerned. I wanted to know how you are doing and to hear it from you."

"I'm doing fine, Michelle, and I don't want you worrying about me right before you skate in the Olympics. I'm going to be all right . . . and, Michelle . . . thanks for the call."

Michelle's was one among hundreds of calls and letters that I received right after that announcement. I was touched that people were so concerned about me. It had something to do with me as a person, for sure, but I guess it also had to do with a reality check for us Baby Boomers. People still had this picture of me in that green dress at the Olympics, or the woman in the wispy costumes gliding through commercials for Canon cameras and Concord watches. Those kinds of people with those kinds of perfect lives didn't get breast cancer, did they? If they did, it was a big reminder that we are all mortal . . . even people who were once teenage girls in green dresses gliding on the ice.

I was deluged with well-wishers and interview requests from reporters, but what I needed was some peace and quiet . . . and that thing that had always gotten my mind off my troubles since I was old enough to walk . . . exercise, preferably with a friend.

Coincidentally, before the word *cancer* had become a daily fixture in my life, my friend Martha and I had been planning a girls-only vacation down at Rancho La Puerta, a health spa south of San Diego, just over the Mexican border . We had a lot of back and forth about whether or not we should go, but between the pressure of phone calls and the responsibility of running the house, I just wanted to escape for a little bit. Greg thought it would be good for me, and Dr. Bertelsen didn't see any reason why I shouldn't go, as long as I was feeling physically okay. So Martha and I were off to Mexico.

I did, however, have a tube sticking out of my body to drain the lymph nodes. It was like a big, thick, messy, awkward, uncomfortable straw, which I had to wear for about ten days before I had healed enough to remove it. I was to have the tube pulled out of me the day before I left, but little did I know how painful it would be. I thought at least they would numb me with something before they pulled it out, but they didn't. The doctor said not to worry, and the nurses said, "Everybody does this. It's nothing. You hardly feel it."

So I was all prepared for something like a penicillin shot. "Okay, count to three. We're going to do it real quick," the doctor promised.

On a scale of one to ten—with delivering a baby being ten and a sore throat being one—this was about an eight.

At last the tube was gone! I felt pretty much like my old self again. I was able to do yoga and at least some stretching with the bandages. Of course I didn't do any big vigorous exercise classes right away. . . . I saved that for the second day.

We went to seminars. We read. We made wreaths out of wild herbs. We played bingo. We had massages and loofa scrubs. It was a complete and welcome change of pace. I had the opportunity to center myself—mentally, physically, and spiritually. I turned to my body the same way that I had when I was a little girl, when I would try to put aside my problems by skating as hard and as much as I could. When you are young, though, the body all works the way it should. Now, as I was hitting fifty, my body, which had always been my salvation, was the problem. So I turned to the problem to fix the problem, which was all I really knew to do.

I turned to the same drive and focus that had always centered me as an athlete. I would have to use them now, not to win a medal but to do whatever it took to heal my body.

Martha was the perfect person to spend this time with. I found out then—and continued to find out—you need friends when you go through something as emotional and serious as breast cancer. Martha and I are both doctor's wives, and as a doctor's wife, I know a little. But back then, that little didn't have much to do with my condition. Martha's husband, Kurt, is an oncologist, so she had some knowledge to share.

So we exercised and had hours and hours of good girl talk, which was very reassuring. The combination of the spa and her friendship were just the right environment to get me in shape to handle all the commotion I would have to face when I returned to the States: my family, the press, and beginning almost as soon as I returned, the radiation treatment.

I entered radiation treatment as if I were preparing for a performance on the ice: I got myself in shape and expected that to take me through without any problems. I fully expected to feel great: I was doing aerobic classes, hiking. I was as fit as a person could be. But a disease doesn't have a mind, or a country, or a team. It doesn't know—or care—how hard you worked at conditioning yourself. It just is. If you are lucky, you beat it. Radiation is just one of the things you do to beat cancer. Having seen what my fellow patients went through, I am glad it was all I had to do.

First they tattoo you. This is definitely not a style thing. They need to do it so that they can line up the radiation with the cancerous area. Then you come back the next day and you start. This particular treatment center was very mindful of my privacy. In fact they didn't need to be. Even though they offered me a private waiting room, I really preferred being in the regular waiting room with the other patients. We were all going through the same thing, and we gave each other a lot of support. We had lots of magazines and puzzles to pass the time and plenty of nice hot tea. We traded war stories. We compared notes on which creams were working to help with the irritation. Radiation therapy is like a major dose of sunburn, and your skin gets very irritated and sensitive. In the case of sunburn, the way around it is simple: You just stay out of the sun. With radiation treatments you can't stay out of the radiation, although one of the women had such a bad reaction that she had to take a rest from the treatments.

About three weeks into the treatments, I started feeling all the classic symptoms: skin discoloration, itching, and fatigue. If there was one time I was glad to be married to a dermatologist, this was it. In addition to being a loving husband, a good listener, and a really supportive friend, Greg knew a thing or two about ointments and creams. He would bring new things home and treat my sensitive areas when I was really down on the whole thing. I would also pass along recommendations to my "radiation friends."

There were two women with whom I became quite close—Anne and Wendy. We became our own support group. If there was one word I would use to describe Wendy, it would be *happy*. She was the most cheerful and upbeat of our little group. When she complained, she did it from a happy place. If she was having a reaction to the radiation, she would find some way to poke fun at it. She was always trying to make a little joke and, boy, was I ever in need of a couple of laughs at that time in my life! Whenever Wendy walked into the radiation waiting room, she would brighten it up. We needed brightening, sitting around in those ugly robes they give you. I mean, when you have breast cancer, you're not usually feeling pretty. They ought to have prettier robes.

Somehow, Wendy could always make the best of it. There I would be, feeling disheveled and definitely unpretty, and Wendy would walk in and light up the whole room. Even more miraculous, Wendy always looked totally put together. I didn't even know she had a wig on until we were a few weeks into treatments. In case you were wondering, I didn't lose my hair, which is often a reaction to chemotherapy—a treatment I didn't receive. Wendy had gone through chemo before she had radiation. Whenever I found myself feeling down I would say to myself, "Gosh, if Wendy can be happy going through this, then how can I feel so sorry for myself?" In the six weeks that we were together in treatment, Wendy was always up and happy.

My other friend, Anne, was quieter than Wendy. Anne and I started talking in the parking lot one day, and we really connected. We ended up standing out there for half an hour, trading stories about our lives and what we were going through. "I don't know if you want to hear this," Anne confided to me, "but I'm a recurrence after thirteen years."

"Oh no!" I said. What else can you say? Actually, I *did* want to hear her story, and I wanted her to hear mine. It was so important to have somebody to talk to, just to get it all out of my system. It was the same for Anne, and it worked for both of us. Anne, Wendy, and I grew very close during those weeks. We would meet for lunch or go out for juice and coffee after the treatments. By unloading on each other, we weren't bringing the whole thing back home to our families.

Anne handled things differently than Wendy. She was positive, but after a recurrence, you tend not to have that attitude of "I can definitely lick this thing." Wendy's high spirits helped us both, but having Anne's honesty helped me to look at the problem truthfully: Yes, I would probably get better and stay better, but no, there are no guarantees. Like everything else in the Long Program of life, you do your best, even when you fall down.

During the first three weeks of my treatment, I was running almost four days a week. I would drop Todd off at school, go for my treatment, talk with my friends a little bit, then go for an hour's run, come back home, shower, and get into my day.

Then it hit me. You can't bombard your body with that many rays without it doing something to you. The fatigue and the irritation hit me, and so did a bout with depression. That was new to me. My dad's death, my mom's death—none of that had brought me this far down.

One of the drugs I was taking to prevent the reoccurrence of my cancer was Tamoxifen, and some of its side effects can be major hot flashes and depression. I didn't know that the drug was making me depressed. I just thought I was down because of the cancer. I mean, if you are going to be down, cancer is about as good a reason as I know.

I started closing down—withdrawing. I have read that depression is like a black cloud descending on you. Mine felt like I was sitting on top of the hill in Los Gatos, watching rain clouds coming in from the ocean, darkening everything. Everything was difficult: the burden of the house, taking Todd to school or helping him with homework—all the things that made life feel right and secure seemed to have lost all their meaning. "Oh, my God," I would think, "how am I ever going to do all this laundry?" Or "I have to shop for groceries *and* make dinner? I just can't face it." Everything was such an effort.

I even cut back on exercise. This was a real telltale sign. All the studies will tell you that exercise helps with depression, and it certainly has been my go-to therapy my whole life, but not this time. Instead of running in the hills with my girlfriends four times a week, I started to go two times and then eventually no times. I went less and less to my trainer, Mark. If I did make it to the gym, I was really tired of everybody trying to cheer me up, telling me, "Oh, we're so proud of you," or "Going through what you're going through and *still* coming to the gym—what a role model!"

They all meant well, but I just didn't want to hear it: not even from my best friends, Jean and Martha, whom I could always talk to. Jean knew something was up when I stopped calling her.

Greg, on the other hand, was an enormous help, the only one I could really talk to. Between helping me through radiation with his medical knowledge and just being there for me as a husband, he was my rock. I wouldn't recommend cancer to anyone as a marriage builder, but one effect it had on mine was to make me realize how deep is his love for me and mine for him. Whatever we had going in got deeper through this ordeal.

One day I said to Greg, "Look, we both know that this isn't like me. It has to be the Tamoxifen." I said that half because I believed it and half because I hoped it was true. "Do you think it would be really risky if I went off it?"

Greg replied, "Actually, I don't, but I am not the cancer specialist. Let's ask your doctor."

This was one of the few times I was a less-than-ideal patient. I took myself off the drug about a week before I went to see the doctor. By the time I went to him I was already feeling more like my old self. He explained to me that, at best, the drug was giving me a two percent better chance of avoiding a recurrence and, all things considered, my quality of life was an important consideration. If I weren't getting all those side effects, of course I would have stayed on it, and if I had a recurrence I would definitely have stayed on it as Anne did—depression, hot flashes, and all.

I felt better and better. The cloud that had rolled in over Los Gatos and parked itself over the Jenkins home began to lift. I felt like exercising again, and I started to run regularly. But even now that I am basically recovered, I'm not quite as dedicated about getting back to the weights and the workouts as I was before. I am still a little worn out from the last year.

After I finished radiation and then stopped taking the drug, I was physically and spiritually a lot better. Still, you always worry, "Am I doing enough to make sure that I stay healthy?" Dr. Porzig, my oncologist, said that feeling is normal. Patients tend to think their cancer will come back when the treatment ends because they are not doing enough. During treatments, you have the sense of doing something proactive to fight the cancer. After treatment, many patients feel as if they're no longer as involved in actively fighting their cancer. Statistically, now, I am no more apt to get cancer than I was before. So, yes, I have to pay attention. But my antennae are now permanently up. If I ever do have a recurrence, I hope I will catch it even earlier.

When I was going through treatments, two of my sisters came to visit with me for a few days. Greg was out of town, so it was just a girls' weekend: Cathy, Max, and Peggy. They wanted to show me love and support and to see that I was okay, and it was a chance for us to have a fun weekend and just be sisters again. We are so busy with our married lives and our kids that we don't make time for that, and if we do get together it is with the kids and husbands, which is a different dynamic. Those few days centered us.

I told them that I would often find myself out and about— at the grocery store, or on some errand—feeling okay, when someone would come up and ask, "How is your cancer doing?"

I told them that it felt as if people kept reminding me that I was sick. I know they wished me the best, but it would have been a whole lot easier on me, or on anybody who has cancer, if people simply said, "I've been thinking about you."

There is no one right thing to say in that situation. But I do know that when you are going through something like this, you want to forget your disease and not be reminded of it.

So I told my sister, "You know what I should do, Max? I

should just wear a hat telling everybody I'm fine. And then people won't feel obliged to ask."

"I'll be glad to stitch that out for you," she offered.

So I bought a baseball hat, and Maxine stitched "I'm Fine" across the front. I loved it, and it occurred to me that Scott Hamilton, who had also gone through cancer treatments, would like one too. Maxine obliged. When I gave it to Scott, I told him the story and he said, "Yeah, I get that a lot too."

But many well-wishers need to be told firsthand that you are okay, which was part of the reason I finally ended up cooperating on a *People* magazine story.

Friends have heard me say that Greg and I aren't *People* magazine people. By that I meant we are not showbiz types. We have always tried to live a normal life in a normal town, without a lot of the glitz and glamour that goes with being in the public eye. So, when *People* called about doing an article, I was not that disposed toward it. When it turned out they were going to do it anyway, I thought I'd tell my own story instead of having someone else do it. I nixed a photo shoot at that time, which coincided with one of my emotional low points, but the story and the response were quite gratifying. I began to hear from many women who were strengthened somewhat by having me go public with my story.

That first brush with *People* in June led to another story—a cover story—about breast cancer survivors. I was through with my treatments but still feeling kind of low. I didn't feel like a star, I didn't feel pretty, and I was intimidated by being included with all those other stars. What I felt was vulnerable and insecure. Still, this group of famous women who had all survived breast cancer would deliver a strong message, and I wanted to do my part, even if I wasn't at my best.

There were more women on the cover than were able to make it to the photo shoot that day. Betty Ford was unable to be there, so she was photographed at a different time and put in the final picture by digital imaging. But we had an interesting group anyway, and it was good for me to talk with the other women about our experiences. Olivia Newton-John was there, as was Diahann Carroll. Marsha Wallace, who played Carol on *The Bob Newhart Show,* was a lot of fun. It was great to talk with Jill Eikenberry, from *L.A. Law.* And then it was a major thrill to meet my mother's idol, Shirley Temple. It was a different feeling than with Anne and Wendy. In addition to sharing breast cancer, the women at the *People* shoot have always been, like myself, in the public eye. We all knew that the same spotlight, which we all loved, shines just as brightly when things aren't going so well, and you're on display at a time when that's the last thing you want. Learning how they all dealt with their ordeals was good for me.

Olivia was relaxed and friendly, pretty much the cheerleader of the group. Whereas I was still a little gun-shy about being back in the spotlight, Olivia was a six-year survivor. Diahann Carroll came in at the last minute—she was still in treatment and yet she looked beautiful. She came in with a mini-entourage including someone who said things like, "Shoot her from this side—it's her best one." They didn't have to worry. She is still a gorgeous lady.

Shirley was a real inspiration. It was twenty-something years since she had been diagnosed, so when she said, "Don't worry, it will all come out fine," we believed her.

Shirley Temple is from the old Hollywood-star school. She was quite definite about what she should wear. She liked what she brought better than the clothes *People* had on hand. I remember her red, red lipstick: very Hollywood, from the glamour days. This is a woman who knows how to be a star.

"I want to be in the middle of the shot," she said, "because that's the star position. They can't cut you out if you're in the middle." And we all said, "Good for you, Shirley! You're in the middle."

While we were sitting around, Shirley talked about her mastectomies. I am so lucky that these days they don't just go and do them the minute you are diagnosed. Shirley said that she wishes she had had reconstructive surgery, but since she's in her seventies, she thought, "Why do it now?" She was very matter-of-fact about it, which is, in the end, the way you have to be. She told stories about how her prosthesis slips every once in a while and it's kind of a pain in the neck, but no worse, she said, than "hitching up your panty hose." Basically she doesn't think about it anymore unless someone asks. It's just her body and she accepts it.

One of the most encouraging things was speaking to women who had it worse than I did, some of whom lost breasts, yet here they were going on with life and doing it well. I felt so lucky that my lumpectomy had left my breast with only a small scar. We broke for lunch and had lots of girl talk, about work, kids, and family. Everybody had a good time and everyone was trying to look their best. That was so good for me at that point.

Then *People* came out to take a picture that would run inside the story. If you look closely at the photo, you will see that I have a messed-up elbow. I am lucky that that is all you see. The day before the shoot, I went for an hour's run on the mountain trail. I must not have been looking, because I stumbled on a rock and did a perfect face plant. I cut my elbow and did a pretty good job on my face too. The face was fixable with makeup, but the elbow was such a mess that I couldn't hide it with makeup. I told the photographer and he said, "Don't worry, they'll retouch it at the magazine."

That phrase, "they'll retouch it," is now one of my candidates for the list of major lies of the century. There am I with Todd on page 86, and my elbow looks like I just came out of a hockey pileup! As I looked at it, the thought crossed my mind that I still have a lot of the old tomboy in me.

All the attention surrounding the *People* cover and the TV and radio appearances that went with it reminded me how sometimes fame enables us to get a positive message out to people who need it. People put athletes on a pedestal of health and fitness, and to hear that an Olympic athlete came down with this kind of disease, especially during the Olympics, gives people a jolt of reality. It says this can happen to anybody, no matter who you are, no matter how fit you are.

I saw the effect of my going public when I appeared on Oprah that May. A few hours before I left to catch my flight to Chicago, I received a phone call from the producers. They wanted to know if I had received any letters that would be interesting to read on the air. I had received a lot, and the hard part was picking one. Finally, Greg reminded me of the story of a woman whose husband had heard the announcement about my cancer when Jim Nantz opened his evening coverage with it.

Apparently the woman had been putting off making an appointment for her mammogram. With three little kids, I can understand how she found little time to squeeze in an appointment. "I'm too busy" was the excuse she gave to her husband. No matter how busy life gets, you need to set priorities.

After the announcement, the husband made an appointment and, sure enough, they found a mass. It was malignant. They operated, and she had a mastectomy and reconstructive surgery, followed by radiation and chemo. She is going to be all right. There are three little children who are going to have their mom around, which I found very moving. Oprah flew them in to be with me in the studio when they taped my visit, and they read their letter to me. Basically, the husband thanked me for saving his wife's life, and he got pretty teary. So did I. So did Oprah. So did the audience.

The moral of the story: Early detection can mean that cancer is not the death sentence it once was. Early detection can save your life. It saved mine.

When you face a crisis like this and come through it, you see life differently. I think my life is a little more organized now because of what I went through. I know what makes me happy. After being depressed during my medical crisis, I know that I am basically a happy person and I want to keep that alive in me. I want to enjoy each day fully, and I realize now that every day is a gift.

I take things more comfortably now. Even as I write this, the old me would have been stressed out about having to pack for a trip to Finland to broadcast the World championships. Now, my attitude is, the packing can wait. It will get done as well as it gets done. If I forget something, so what? Life goes on.

I remember the day that I started to feel good again and went for my first long run around the reservoir. I think I ran for an hour and a half because I felt so happy. I was just going to go do a little run, but my friends, Jeannie and

Jerilynn, asked if I wanted to try the long trail, which I hadn't done in weeks.

"Sure," I said. "I feel okay. Let's do it." I got to the top of the hill over by the dam, and I could see our house. I just stood there. "Wow," I thought, "I am fine—more than fine. I feel great."

Of course, life never lets you coast for too long that way. In my case, it was eight weeks. That's when Andy called me about Jamaica and their upcoming baby. Just when I had pulled through one thing, here came another one right around the corner. I guess the Long Program is always that way; there is always something around the next corner, something to deal with. At this stage of the game, I've learned it's how you deal with it that counts.

For a Longer Program

I t may sound obvious, but your own Long Program will be around only as long as you are. You can make the best personal and career decisions, but without good health, they are not going to do you much good. Your genetic makeup is out of your control, but eating well and staying fit are completely up to you. Pay attention to them, and you will live longer and more fully.

Even though I have made fitness a part of my life since I was very young, I am not one of those people who think that fitness and nutrition will save you from everything. Even before I got cancer, I remember how this point was tragically driven home with the death of Sergei Grinkov in 1995. If anyone ever looked as strong and vigorous as a bull, it was Sergei. And yet, at the age of 28, he was dead of a heart attack. It shook up the entire skating world, and it seriously scared me. My father had three heart attacks by the time he died at forty one, so I know that heart disease isn't just something that happens to older people.

When Sergei died, I asked a cardiologist friend if, given my family history, I should be looked at. "Absolutely, and bring Andy when you do." So we had our mother/son stress test and, thankfully, everything was fine. But Sergei's death and my cancer should be a lesson: The fittest people succumb to the same ailments that couch potatoes get. If you do get sick in spite of staying fit and eating right, you can't think, "Oh, what's the use of staying in shape if this happened?" It is important to remember that your reserves of strength and conditioning can help you fight disease.

I wasn't born fit and I wasn't born an ice skater. I became those things largely by accident, with a little help from heredity and my family's culture thrown in. The physical fitness part of my family heritage started with my grandfather, Harry Deal. Until he died at age eighty-nine, he walked two miles every day of his life. It was Grandpa who told me that you need to participate, to jump into life, or you would lose your enthusiasm for living. Years before Nike came out with its "Just Do It" ads, Grandpa was living it—and for sure, it rubbed off on me.

On walks with my grandpa, or by myself, I always liked being outside in the fresh air. As a child, I would climb every tree that had a limb that I could reach. My mom used to tell a story about how, at age four, I went all the way to the top of a redwood tree at our house in the Santa Cruz mountains. I was having a ball up there, but Mom and Dad were scared. Rather than climbing the tree to rescue me, Dad told me how to do it myself: "Take one branch at a time. Look at that next branch. Don't look all the way down. One branch at a time going down, the same way you did it when you went up."

One step at a time. Look at the next step, not at the last step.

I think that piece of advice is the one I took most to heart as an athlete and as a woman trying to keep family, career, and my body together at the same time.

If I were born a boy, I don't believe that things would have turned out the same. When I was quite young I played baseball with the boys, but a girl could go just so far in team sports. The schools weren't set up with programs to encourage us. For that matter, society didn't encourage girls to become active in sports the way boys are practically required to be. A boy who didn't play team sports in my childhood was an oddity. A girl, on the other hand, could do quite well socially without ever throwing a ball or running a step.

Skating was different. Boys and girls could both do it. It didn't have a whole culture of teams. For me, skating was like running outside, or climbing trees, or swinging on the monkey bars: I was my whole team, so to speak, and I loved it. Skating got me into a lifetime of solo sports that never failed to get my adrenaline pumping. That same rush was certainly the main attraction when I started to drive fast cars. I liked the challenge of being the fastest, the first, the best.

That challenge is something inside you. It's what made me get my certification as a scuba diver. As a child, I had loved the ocean, but as I grew older, I began to develop a fear of it, in the same way that some people can, all of a sudden, become fearful in an airplane. By the time the movie, *Jaws,* came out, my fear became terror. Finally I said to myself, "This is just plain silly!" I chose to face my fear head-on and take a scuba diving course with some friends.

Some fears you never overcome, but some you can stare down until they back off. If you don't like anxieties—and I don't know anyone who does—facing them is the best way to overcome them. When you do, there is often a new source of joy and strength hiding behind that fear.

With ice skating, it was a pure joy at the beginning. Later it became a job—but it was always one that I felt lucky to have. Becoming a skater meant that I practiced hours and hours every day. That discipline is something that has carried over into my "normal" life of trying to stay fit.

One of the most important things to keep in mind for being healthy is that you have to both make time and steal time. By making time I mean you have to get into a routine and follow it. Whether you have a group of friends or a personal trainer, most of us need other people to give us the impetus to stay on course.

Even the most disciplined person will have to skip a day, or even a few days, of exercise sometimes. That's life and that's why you have to steal time when you can. When you have the ability to get in a concentrated period of daily exercise, seize it. Don't believe what you hear about exercising one day and not exercising the next . Exercise whenever you can.

When I was training for the Olympics, I put in four, five, and six hours every day of strenuous exercise. So when I hear people say, "I shouldn't run today—I worked too hard yesterday, and I need to give my body a rest," my answer is, "Who says so?" I trained long hours *every* day. All athletes do. It's not killing us—in fact, it is what makes us better. It builds strength, endurance, and consistency. If I held to the day-of-training/day-of-rest theory, I would never have won the Olympics.

The ad says, "Just do it," but it doesn't say, "Just overdo it." It is one thing to train hard and consistently, but it's another to push your body beyond where it can go. If you pay attention to the small injuries and the first feelings of aches and pains, you are less likely to experience more serious problems. The more you exercise, the more you know how your body feels and the more attuned you are to things that aren't right. If my knee starts to hurt when running, I'll slow down or stop—and then I'll shake out the cramp or walk it off. If you get a blister, deal with it right away: Put a Band-Aid on it, or just stop running until you can get to a bandage. Little injuries and pains rarely become big ones if you pay attention to them. I am quite proud of the fact that I have never had a serious sports injury—if you don't count the time when I was six and fell while running down a hill when Mom called for dinner. I needed ten stitches. Accidents happen to the best of us, but being mindful of aches and pains is one of the best pieces of conditioning advice I can give.

I have tried all kinds of things to stay in shape. I've done aerobics and still do occasionally. The dancing, the music, and the people all made exercising easier. As with so much else in sports, group energy is a great motivator. It was not that different from skating practice in certain ways: music and friends and all of us feeling the peer pressure to excel. It's very easy to fall off the exercise wagon when you are home alone and don't feel like making the effort, but when you are part of a group, it's harder to make those same excuses to your classmates. A call from a friend is often the little extra motivator you need to get out the door.

I run as often as I can with a group of friends. We meet down by the beginning of a trail that climbs away from the freeway and makes a circuit through the hills. A few weeks ago we had a spell of really bad weather: cold and rainy. One friend called and said maybe the weather was just too rotten to run, and I kind of agreed. Then my friend Jeannie, who is also a member of our group, called and said, "I'm feeling so flabby that I just can't stand it. We've *got* to run." So we skipped the muddy trail and kept to the streets in town, and I went from not feeling like running to feeling great. I just needed somebody to jump-start me. We all do.

Even though Greg and I are both keen on keeping ourselves fit, in our case, husband-and-wife fitness works better if we keep it separate. We tried exercising together, and it didn't work that well. He is bigger, stronger, and faster than I am. When we tried running together, he was always way ahead of me and would get antsy that I was going so slow. Greg is also much more fanatic about working out than I am. On weekends I might want to sleep in while he's up and out of the house for a two-hour workout, rowing his single scull on the Lexington Reservoir. By the time he gets home, gets showered, gets dressed, and has a bite, it's ten A.M. That's the way Greg approaches fitness. He looks great and I am all for it, but I am not that way.

I want to stay healthy and stay in shape and then get on with the rest of my life. As life goes on, I need to remind myself that my body is changing and so are my fitness requirements.

With every passing year our metabolism changes so that more of what we eat seems to attach itself to those places where we least need the extra weight. The metabolism slows down, the lean muscle mass diminishes, and the weight goes up. There are only two ways to control the process: nutrition and activity.

Aerobic activity—running, walking, StairMaster, dancing— is a critical element in any fitness program. But in terms of getting your body to look the way you would like it to look, women are starting to enjoy the benefits of weight training, which used to be something that most women associated with muscle-bound guys. That is not really the case. If you want to look like a female Arnold Schwarzenegger, that's up to you—and it's difficult to achieve unless you pump iron several hours a day. Lifting weights can also make a woman look more sculpted, yet more smooth. It can also help increase your metabolism.

Cindy, the friend whom I did the scuba diving with, thought a good next project would be to try weight lifting. I thought "good idea" since I was feeling kind of soft after Todd was born. Firming up and losing some weight were at the top of my personal wish list. Shortly after we started, Cindy injured herself and stopped lifting, but I kept at it. I could really see the difference in my body. Early on in my weight-training regime, I worked out with a female trainer while Greg worked out with a guy trainer. After our session he and I would go out to dinner. It's always nice to go out for a bite after you have worked out. You feel you deserve a good meal. It also worked out as a perfect "date night" for Greg and me.

I had been lifting for two or three years when I met Mark Fredericks, the trainer I've been with the longest. Mark has worked with a lot of people who have my kind of erratic schedule, and he has been able to adjust. It has been a much deeper and more rewarding learning experience than I ever expected it to be when we started. I already knew a little about weight training, having done all kinds of exercise for years, and I felt that I ate correctly instinctively. But what I learned from Mark was the whole package: a combination of aerobic exercise with an emphasis on achieving the right heart rate, strengthening and shaping through weight training, and good nutrition. It's like a circle, one thing influencing the other.

If one of your goals is staying at a good weight, the basic law of nature is you cannot take in more calories than you expend. There are only two ways to control this: eat fewer calories and/or burn more calories through activity. Like any good trainer, Mark opts for a two-pronged attack. In terms of burning calories, the only way to do it is to get your heart rate up. You can see how effectively you are doing that if you buy one of those heart-rate monitors you find at stores that sell running gear, cycling stuff, etc. They cost under a hundred dollars and you just strap it on and it reads out your heart rate as you go. It's a terrific device because in addition to giving you useful information, it also gives you something to do while you're putting in those long miles. You get your heart rate up to a high enough speed so that you begin burning the fuel you have stored as fat. This doesn't mean you have to run the marathon, but it does mean you have to put in the time.

For my age and body weight, the ideal heart rate is between 125 and 150 beats per minute. If I run, I keep it closer to 150. If I walk fast and swing my arms, I'm closer to 130. It's not all that strenuous. The trick is to do it for an hour. If you can find the hour, you can do it.

I walk and run up and down some of the hilly streets in our town, or I take a four-mile path through the hills. One way to make sure you put in an hour is to park your car and run or walk for a half hour before you turn back. That way you have to put in the whole hour to get your car back.

When I am on the road, I will do my best to give forty-five minutes to the treadmill or, if possible, go for a run. If it's a non-state-of-the-art hotel or a place like Finland in the middle of the winter, I'll walk up and down the stairs for twenty minutes. Bottom line, I always try to do something. In addition to burning calories, aerobic exercise strengthens your heart. If you've been a couch potato for years and haven't done any exercise, you should see your doctor before you start a serious exercise program. He or she will probably recommend a stress test first, depending on your age and overall health.

I don't have to tell you to make sure your heart beats while you exercise—your body does that automatically. Breathing, though, seems to be something that we have to relearn when we exercise. You tend to hold your breath when you get tense, and that is often the time that your muscles want the extra oxygen. This is a point that Mark emphasizes when I started to get into bad habits doing leg presses. I would hold my breath sometimes and really give an "oommph" as I pushed on the weights with my legs.

"You need *more* oxygen now, not less," he said. "Keep breathing."

He was right. I was amazed how much more energy I had after a few cleansing breaths.

That's one argument for having a personal trainer. A good one will be so in tune with you that he or she will notice things that you may miss while you concentrate on your workout. Of all people, I should have remembered proper breathing technique because I had been taught proper breathing when I was a young skater. My teachers knew that competition as a rule makes people nervous, and when that happens, you forget to breathe. When you do that, you can tire in the first minute of a routine, which is pretty much of a guarantee that you will run out of steam well before the end. Even after all those years of competition, when I started with a serious exercise program, those lessons turned out not to be so ingrained, and I had to learn them all over again.

When my life is calmer—in other words when I am not on the road and there isn't too much going on at home—I try to exercise a lot, because I know that life never stays calm for too long. Pretty soon there will be other demands on me. Some people get up early and get their exercise in before the rest of the household gets in gear. Having gone to the rink before dawn all those years, I am no longer eager to leap out of bed at six for a full workout. I prefer to get breakfast together for Greg and Todd and send them off on their day and then get down to the business of my workout. If I don't do it then, I know I will get lazy and make excuses. By the afternoon I will feel like an absolute slug with no motivation to exercise. So usually I will go for a run with my girlfriends, and then before I come home lift weights for forty-five minutes. Three, four, and sometimes five times a week I will work with Mark at the gym, and those are full workouts.

When I can get myself on that kind of schedule for a few weeks, I can see my body take shape and I feel great. Now I know it's not realistic for any mom who also has a career to think she can keep up that kind of a program all the time, but even when I have to cut back, I make myself do enough so that the basic body maintenance is done when I want to get back into a fuller exercise schedule.

Mark also put me and five of his other clients through his "Fitness Boot Camp"—an intensive four-day workout program, a regimen he developed for swimsuit models who had upcoming shoots and wanted to slim down and firm up. When Mark told me about it, I had no problem wanting to look like a swimsuit model.

For those four days, Mark ordered our food, told us when to eat and what to do. We started at eight in the morning with an aerobics class. Then we'd drink plenty of water and go for a long run followed by weight training. Then we'd go out for lunch, which Mark ordered, keeping the carbohydrates down because the body turns them into fat easily. After a rest, we did a long fast walk, and then some weight training, finishing up with an hour on the stationary bikes. It wasn't nonstop: we took short breaks all through the day, but it was a lot of exercise. There were a few complainers in the group, but we all made it through. As the big-time athlete in the bunch, I never let out a peep in protest. I was a big cheerleader: "You can do this," I would say or—better—show by example. At the end of the four days, everybody had taken a few inches off in the right places.

Boot camp is no substitute for a regular exercise program, but when you have a short-term weight-loss and fitness goal, it's great. Lots of trainers have similar courses or can set one up if you inquire. But whatever you do, don't let the question of having a personal trainer hold you back from exercise. A trainer is great, but the really important thing is to simply do something.

One of the great motivators for an exercise program is weight—as in "I could stand to take off a little weight." This has certainly been true for me. When the waistband gets a little tight and my size 8 body has trouble getting into my size 4 or 6 dress, I know one of two things is probably true: I haven't been exercising, or I've been eating too much—or at least, too much of the wrong things.

When I first became an athlete, people didn't know as much as they do today about the relationship between nutrition and fitness. It was more a matter of eating the basic food groups as we learned them back then. I think my mom had an instinctive sense of what is good to eat for athletes though, and she instilled that in me. When we had our little farm in Morgan Hill, there were fresh eggs, vegetables from the garden (organic vegetables, come to think of it), and good meat from our livestock (including the pig that our Doberman killed).

Mom was into healthy things like wheat germ—which she always doled out in mounds on top of our Cream of Wheat in the morning. She was also way ahead of the curve on vitamins—we took tons of them when I was young. I didn't eat a lot of bread as a kid, nor did I go in much for desserts, but I always had a weakness for cinnamon rolls. Whenever I indulged, however, it would show immediately in the tight skating costumes I used to wear and I would begin to feel sluggish on the ice.

I remember putting on a good seven or eight pounds right after I won my gold medal. After all those years of practice, I had reached the pinnacle and, for the first time since I was nine years old, I just kicked back and relaxed. We finally had a little money from my post-Olympic skating and my first TV pay check. We moved from Colorado and I bought a house for us complete with the ultimate luxury, our own swimming pool. We threw lots of parties, had lots of fun, ate more than normal, and I didn't skate as much. The results were predictable: seven pounds more of Peggy Fleming.

I didn't like the way I looked or felt, so I cut out the cinnamon rolls, and went back to salads and protein. Mom was insistent that I have my protein at every meal, just the way Mark is a stickler for that today. Pretty soon my weight was where I wanted it to be. But it's harder to take those pounds off today, which is why I am more careful about what I eat.

Like most American women, I like being thin, or at least the idea of being thin but I never have been obsessed with weight. I am lucky in that respect. I have seen the thin obsession take its toll on many young girls, especially athletes. A skater or a gymnast is *supposed* to be thin. There seems to be a general pre-conception that this is the ideal body type.

Carlo was well aware of this, and his way of letting his students know that he thought they needed to take the pounds off was not particularly gentle. He was naturally blunt in his criticisms, and whatever gentleness he might have had in his native Italian was lost when it came out in his broken English. The result was often somewhat rougher than he probably intended.

The effects were very painful for one of the skaters I was very close with. Carlo told her she would never get to the next level of skating until she did something about her weight. In the way that a sensitive young girl often will, she felt absolutely horrible, and a little bit angry—at herself and at Carlo. She made up her mind to show him that she had the willpower for success. The problem was that her way to show him was by losing an unhealthy amount of weight, and she became bulimic. Fortunately for her, she eventually overcame it. Not every young athlete does.

Bulimia and anorexia were—and for the most part still are—the hushed-up secrets of women's sports. It is so important to be on the lookout for this behavior with girl athletes. It's equally important that we recognize that not everyone can have an ideal body type, but everyone can benefit from taking part in sports. Young girls are so sensitive about their bodies, especially in their teenage years. A little baby fat can last well into adolescence. We shouldn't make a big thing of it. We should encourage athletic participation and a healthy diet, and the weight will take care of itself. We should also watch out for athletic girls who weigh a bit more than "normal" when they put on muscle mass. If they start obsessing about being over their "normal" weight range, dieting trouble can start.

Eating the right things can help at any stage in life. Working with Mark, I have cut way back on my carbohydrates. Athletes have known for a long time that "loading up on carbs" is a way to store fuel that can quickly be converted to energy. Mom and I knew that instinctively when I was a young competitor: In addition to being a champion skater, I was a champion consumer of macaroni and cheese—it was the only thing I could eat before competition. I was often so nervous I couldn't keep anything else down. Carlo tells the story of running out to a Berkley, California, grocery store before the 1966 National Championships to find me macaroni and cheese.

Although carbohydrate loading may be good for athletic competition, I learned as I worked with Mark that if you eat carbohydrates as a way to avoid fats, the body will turn those carbohydrates into fat faster and more efficiently than it will do with any other food. Mark favors protein and lots of *green* vegetables as a way to get the fuel the body needs without the fat. Other vegetables such as potatoes and even carrots turn out to have lots of carbs in the form of natural sugars.

Cutting out fattening desserts—another commonsense weight-control method—hasn't been that much of a struggle for me, but cutting down on carbohydrates means cutting down on bread, and I love bread—especially sourdough bread with lots of butter. The only way I have been able to cut back on bread is simply to stop buying it. For this particular diet advice, I give the credit to my friend Martha.

Martha is a terrific cook and her cupboards are always filled with nutritious foods.

"My theory," she told me, "is that when you go to the grocery store you should be proud of the groceries that go across the checkout line."

At first, I thought that Martha—who has been so much of a role model to me as a wife, mom, and woman—had gone over the edge, starting to sound like a cross between Martha Stewart and Tony Robbins.

"The way I look at it," she explained, "when you go shopping, stay away from the junk food and the things that are tempting you, because once you get home, if they are not there you can't eat them. And if you really want them, you have to get in the car and go to the store, and you are less likely to do that."

I have yet to experience a sense of pride about a bagful of lettuce and chicken breasts, but Martha's anti-munchie method has turned out to be good advice.

People associate me with fitness and I have a kind of next-door-neighbor personality, so ever since I won my Olympic medal, I've been asked to be a spokesperson for different foods. Among the first was California Raisins—before the dancing raisins commercials. I'm sure, if someone had thought of it, they would have asked me to skate around in a raisin suit. I am a good sport and probably would have done it . . . provided, of course, that it was a tasteful and flattering raisin costume.

I have never been a health food evangelist nor did I ever follow an "athlete's diet," even in my competition years. The only thing I have always insisted on is that the food be healthy. I always tried to eat what common sense would tell you is healthy. Raisins were, and are, a healthy snack and Americans like raisins.

Pork is a different story. When I went to work for the National Pork Producers Council, pork had a bad rap. People thought it was fatty, and it was against Jewish and Islamic traditions. In the late eighties, no meat was terribly fashionable. People blamed meat for everything that was wrong with the American diet.

I loved pork and always did, going way back to the days when we raised pigs in our little farm in Morgan Hill. I signed on and received a crash course in pork: I learned that it isn't that fatty in relation to other meats, and I was taught how to field questions about all the old wive's tales about pork and pigs. Then I went out to country fairs and supermarkets, met lots of wonderful people, and ate a lot of pork.

At the beginning of my reign as pork spokesperson, I became pregnant with Todd, and my resulting weight elicited a lot of winks and nods from my friends in skating and broadcasting. I took a lot of ribbing—no pun intended—for "the other white meat" as we called it, but it was a fun experience. The bonuses were some recipes that I still make to this day, including a delicious marinated tenderloin with honey and sesame seeds.

Diet and physical exercise on the one hand and strong family life on the other are the cornerstones of my life. They always have been. You cannot separate them, but I am who I am because of the exercise part—in particular, the sport of figure skating. It built my confidence, it conditioned me, and tested me in so many ways: physically, emotionally, and intellectually.

Although any avid sportsperson will say the same thing about his or her sport, to my way of thinking, skating adds even more to the equation. It hones your aesthetic sense, your musical inclinations, your talent for dance, and—from hair and makeup to wardrobe—it allows you to express your personal style. Skating is a supremely expressive sport.

I didn't take it up, nor did I pursue it, to make it my career. I just loved sports as a young girl. When I was young, girls and sports—certainly girls and sports careers—didn't often go together. Times have changed, and I am happy about that. It is wonderful to see so many girls and women participating in all levels of sports. It is equally wonderful to see society taking notice and applauding.

Sports are a lifetime source of satisfaction and good health. I may not be able to do as much as I could when I was younger—I'm slowing down and I have less drive than I once did—but I will always do something to stay fit.

You need to be here to get through your Long Program. Maintaining your fitness and health is one way to make sure you stay here. Family and those you love, that's the other way. With them, you may slip and fall on the ice and not every jump will earn a perfect six, but the real Long Program isn't about perfection. It's about being ready for change and welcoming change for the good it can bring. We all fall down, but as I learned so well as a little girl in a big spotlight: Get up and keep on going. Don't look back. Keep your eyes on the ice.

You can do it!

Awards and Titles

Awards

1967 ABC Athlete of the Year

1968 Babe Didrikson Zaharias Award

1974 AGVA Entertainer of the Year for Special Entertainment

United States Figure Skating Association Hall of Fame

U.S. Olympic Hall of Fame

State of Colorado Hall of Fame

Women's Sports Foundation Hall of Fame

Bay Area Sports Hall of Fame

San Jose Sports Hall of Fame

1994 Sports Illustrated 40th Anniversary "40 for the Ages" Honor

National Service Leadership Award from the National Osteoporosis Foundation

1997 USOC Olympic Spirit Award

Competitive Career Championship Titles
United States National Championships:
1964 Cleveland, Ohio
1965 Lake Placid, New York
1966 Berkeley, California
1967 Omaha, Nebraska
1968 Philadelphia, Pennsylvania

World Championships:
1966 Davos, Switzerland
1967 Vienna, Austria
1968 Geneva, Switzerland

Olympic Winter Games:
1968 Grenoble, France

As they always say, this book could not have been possible without the help of the following people. In my case, this *life* could not have been possible without their help.

My two sons, Andy and Todd—for giving me a joy I never knew existed. Nothing could have ever prepared me for this love, for this pride, for the full life my children have given me.

My sisters, Janice, Maxine, and Cathy—for their sacrifices, especially as children. I can never make up for those years of Mom's absence because of me, but I know now what a hardship it was. You've always been there for me, and I am so grateful for your support.

My dad, whose time with us was far too short—for his infectious enthusiasm for sports even while working so hard to make ends meet, and for taking me to that ice rink when I was nine years old.

Bob Banner—for seeing a future none of us imagined. In the rough world of show business, he is a true gentleman with a clear vision.

Lee Mimms—for fifteen years of creative management and a special friendship. His loyalty, humor, and imagination helped me find a balance. He truly understood all the sides of my family.

My ABC family, past and present, but especially: Roone Arledge, Brian Boitano, Dick Button, Kathy Cook, Joel Feld, Curt Gowdy, Jr., Terry Gannon, Bob Iger, Bill Kunz, Meg Streeter Lauck, Dennis Lewin, Jim McKay, Al Michaels, Julie Moran, Jack O'Hara, Robin Stratton Rivera, Norm Samet, Chris Schenkel, Lydia Stephans, Dennis Swanson, Lesley Visser, Doug Wilson, and Nancy Stern Winters.

Jean Hall—for being a wonderful personal assistant for the past eight years. But most importantly, for being a steady friend and companion for twenty-five years. Your humor, honesty (I know you'll tell me if my butt looks too big), and love have meant so much.

My present management team at IMG: Barry Frank, Jay Ogden, Deb Nast, and especially Sue Lipton, whose tireless dedication keeps it all running. Her professionalism and personal warmth are a rare and wonderful combination.

Acknowledgments

My collaborator, Peter Kaminsky—for his patience and perspective. His rich background of talents has made him the literary Zamboni on the rutted ice of this book project. Thank you for smoothing the way.

Carlo Fassi—for providing the final link. His coaching skill, gentle manner, and confident guidance were a perfect match for my mom and me. Three people won the Olympic gold medal on February 10, 1968; Peggy and Doris Fleming, and Carlo Fassi.

Bob Paul—for his unending loyalty, patience, and creativity (even when my mother was telling him to put in those little toe turns *again*), and for his lifelong friendship.

The Broadmoor Hotel and especially Thayer Tutt—for their support and encouragement. The beautiful World Arena was an ideal setting to inspire a young athlete. My Colorado years were truly a gift.

Dick Foster—for his talent and hard work on Concert on Ice and my TV specials.

Phyllis and David Kennedy—for showing me, and especially my mother, such kindness over the years.

Martha Neumann—for laughter, advice, understanding, and the most enduring friendship in my life.

All my coaches: Peter Betts, Tim Brown, Carlo Fassi, Bill Kipp, Harriet Lapish, John Nicks, Bob Paul, Doryann Swett, Bob Turk, and Gene Turner. You each made a difference. Thank you.

Mary Goldblatt and Amy Fisher—for always being there for my mother and me.

Mitchell Ivers of Pocket Books, for his unwavering enthusiasm during this project.

Mark Reiter of IMG Literary—for his confidence in me. His knowledge of the publishing world guided us through all the twists and turns of actually producing a book.

Marion Rosenfeld—for her dedication to hours and hours of research on all the details.

Michelle Yung—for backing Mark up.

Harlick Boot Company—for providing me with beautiful skates throughout the years.

Colorado College—for their pride in my accomplishments. There will always be a special place in my heart for the campus where I first fell in love with that young pre-med student.

Ice Follies, Ice Capades, and Holiday on Ice—for all those years on tour that built character and endurance. I have wonderful memories.

All the skaters over the years who've brought me joy and inspiration, from the ice and from the booth. It is impossible for me to name you all.

I am so grateful to all of you. Thank you for being a part of my life.

Index